I0436904

Sometimes Marriage Really Sucks

Sometimes Marriage Really Sucks

(A Wife's Point of View)

Essay Young

Copyright © 2012 by Essay Young.

Library of Congress Control Number: 2012923025
ISBN: Hardcover   978-1-4797-6132-6
                     Softcover   978-1-4797-6131-9
                     Ebook   978-1-4797-6133-3

All rights reserved. No part of this book may be reproduced or transmitted in
any form or by any means, electronic or mechanical, including photocopying,
recording, or by any information storage and retrieval system, without
permission in writing from the copyright owner.

This book was printed in the United States of America.

To order additional copies of this book, contact:
Xlibris Corporation
1-888-795-4274
www.Xlibris.com
Orders@Xlibris.com
117792

Contents

This book is dedicated to my husband Ken and my three children; Doug, Pam and Sarah. They bring value and meaning to my life.

Preface

This short book is not a self-help book. It is not a how-to book. I am not a Ph.D. I have no credentials except as Mrs. or maybe Mom. This is just me and my husband's story, a story of two unimportant people, important only to ourselves and our loved ones, and how two ordinary people can still stay together even in a day and age where it is easy to move on and quit the hard work of a relationship.

This book is also simply what the cover says. It's about marriage from a wife's point of view. I realize that sounds one sided but I can't write from a husband's point of view since I am not the husband, therefore I'm writing for the wife, which I am. There really is no lesson to be learned or any great meaning or message written on these pages. It is purely for the enjoyment of the reader, or perhaps for their annoyance. My thoughts on marriage or mainly my thoughts on my own marriage are something you, as the reader may be able to relate to, to laugh at, or to just plain say "I know, me too!"

I have been married to the same man for 26 years and have a variety of anecdotes, stories, and even questions about marriage. Why are we even together after all these years when we've done and said so many stupid things to each other?

There are no answers in my book. The question of why our marriage has been successful is something I ask myself every time my husband and I fight. I have some assumptions and I may or may not be correct in them. However or whatever the true answer might be, I do concede that we have a great and awesome history of life together and that we've created three great and awesome human beings together in our children. We were truly meant to be together, even with all of our bumps and bruises created daily with our trials and errors. This is how humans learn. I hope you enjoy my story . . .

Acknowledgements/References

In Chapter 10, I used the following reports and articles for my information regarding law enforcement and divorce rates. Please read these in their entirety for complete and accurate information.

1. The Washington Post, September 19, 2010. "Study breaks down Divorce by Occupation" by Ellen McCarthy, Washington Post Staff Writer.
2. The Police Chief Magazine, vol LXXVI, no.1, January 2009. "Law Enforcement Healthy Marriage Family Project" by Gary Westphal, Chief of Police (retired) Mesquite Texas and Linda Openshaw, Associate Professor of Social Work, Texas A&M University—Commerce.
3. "Divorce Rates for Law Enforcement Personnel: Another Myth bites the Dust." Study by Shawn P. McCoy and Michael G. Aamodt, Radford University, October 2008.

Chapter One

Why does he do that?

Do you ever have those days when you wonder just "what the heck am I doing with my life married to this middle-aged adolescent"? As a young girl, I read books and watched movies about Prince Charming, dreamed about the latest hunk on TV or in music, or even imagined a relationship like my mom and dad's. Reality said "who are you kidding? and "let me laugh at you now". At least I thought I would get this guy who was the ideally perfect man (like when we were dating?). He would be extremely intelligent, able to handle any situation with a quick decision, chivalrous, patient, loving, kind, attentive, and of course gorgeous! I could just be a princess on a pedestal. Why not? It works on TV and in the fairytales—it must be reality somewhere, isn't it?

Instead of the perfect ideal man, I got "I'm-keeping-her-in-a-constant-state-of-confusion" man. He says he doesn't want me to mother him and then gets mad when I don't tuck him in bed. He tells me not to nag him about finishing the fence in the backyard and then he reminds me five times to get more milk because we're almost out—who's the nag? He says he doesn't want to see a movie and then is upset when the kids and I go see one without him. He doesn't make sense to me sometimes. And they say women are confusing. Was it a man that said that?

Don't get me wrong. Most of the time he's the perfect partner for me—my best friend. How else could we have made it these last 26 years of marriage? We love the same books and movies, we think alike about politics, religion, same sex marriage (and having the same sex each night doesn't have to be boring!). We have great conversations—even great arguments. He's a caring father to our three children and he works hard at his job. But the best part and what always keeps us together is that we have a tremendous love and respect for each other.

So why does he have to act like a putz and stay mad about the smallest thing and when I apologize too early, will blow me off until I become mad again? Then he's over it but now I don't want to make up. Why does marriage really suck some days?

Well I believe it all started when God decided that there should be two sexes. What for? Didn't he know that it would just lead to a lot of fighting and yelling? He made Adam and then Eve, from a rib taken out of Adam no less. Well we're still fighting for ownership of that rib. And we all know that ribs are best barbequed. And that they're very messy. Do you get the picture? We were destined to fight and be at each other from the beginning of humanity.

My husband works long hours in a heavy uniform with a belt that has an array of heavy objects and tools of his trade dangling from it. No, he's not a plumber (I wish, better pay!), he's a cop and let's face it, a cop is expected to perform the riskiest of jobs and be able to maneuver deftly and quickly all the while carrying an extra 30lbs packed around his frame. It's like a plumber or a carpenter wrapping most of his tool chest around his body and running through the house. Not too comfortable. Plus my husband has to deal with the dregs of society on a daily basis. So yes, I do understand when he comes home really crabby sometimes.

Top this off with the fact that a cop's pay usually sucks so that they all work some kind of off-duty uniformed police security work as a part-time job to help make ends meet—pay for kid's college tuition, alimony, child support, a second mortgage, car loans, or if you're us, just the monthly bills (because I really suck at financial management and keeping us on a budget, I know).

When my husband works a part-time job to help earn extra cash after his regular work shift, he may have a 16 hour work day. I have to be extremely patient with him after these days. Sometimes he wants to eat when he gets home and sometimes he wants to go straight to bed. If he wants to eat something when he gets home and I have nothing prepared for him, he'll get angry. I can say "it'll take me only five minutes to heat up leftovers" and he'll say "don't bother" and go to bed angry. If I have something ready for him when he walks in the door, he'll say "not tonight, I'm too tired". Then I'll be angry. It's a vicious cycle.

So how do I know when he's angry at me at night (sometimes a fight is not obvious to me—like I don't know we're in the middle of one—maybe I'm a little dense that way)? I'll know because he won't leave a light on for me in the bedroom. I'll know because he won't touch me in bed all night or allow me to touch him (I call this one "bed tag" or "cooties". If I touch him, he'll jerk away.). I'll know because he'll lie as far away from my side of the bed as possible—which was a really good trick back when we had to sleep in just a full-sized bed. I'll know because when he gets up in the morning for work the next day, he'll quietly get showered, dressed, and leave without a good-bye kiss to me. This last one is always the clincher. All other previous events may not transpire but if the good-bye kiss doesn't happen, well then he's pissed at me. You know, sometimes marriage really sucks.

The hardest thing to deal with by far is the fact that we cannot make up until he's ready. He says I don't respect the fact that he needs time to cool off. So while he's enjoying a couple of days of vacation from his wife, I'm stuck with a couple of days of suppressed anger and monosyllabic answers. When he's angry, he may or may not eat supper. He may or may not sleep in our bed. Of course, in all fairness, neither may I.

And then we'll make up and everything's wonderful again. He's loving and attentive. He rubs my back and my feet—he'll even **kiss** my feet (yuck! I have ugly feet.). He'll tell me I'm beautiful and that he can't imagine life without me. He'll say he doesn't know how he could ever be mad at me. And then I love him so very much that I know I could never be without him. And I'm reminded again of the man I married.

I married a man that was my best friend. We did everything together in college. We never argued. We agreed about everything. We apologized immediately if we said anything off-color to each other. We totally valued each other's opinion. And then we decided to date each other. We still never argued. We still agreed about almost everything. And then we got married. And then things changed.

My husband is a man that is easily distracted especially when there's a chore that desperately needs to be done—like right now. He always finds some goofy thing to do instead. We may have company coming and the lawn really needs mowing. I'm scrubbing bathrooms and the drain is clogged. I look for him all over the yard to help me, but he's not there. I find him standing in front of the garage installing a wireless keypad for the garage doors. "It's so cool! I didn't know it was wireless?!" I'm not impressed. He's baffled by my reaction. I give him **the look**. He mows the lawn. And now he's thinking "Man, sometimes marriage really sucks". It goes both ways.

Now why is it that every time my husband simply picks up a tool to begin a project he starts to curse and swear? Actually it starts before this when he's still looking for the tool. Actually it starts as soon as he thinks about looking for the tool to begin a project. Oh let's admit it, it just keeps getting sooner and sooner each time. And then he goes to the next phase of accusing the kids of stealing his tools. Why would they steal his tape measure? And the language that comes out of his mouth could make flowers wilt and milk curdle. I immediately learned to make myself scarce when he goes out to work on the car. His swearing builds to a crescendo by the time he's actually working on the car. But when he's done, he's whistling and smiling and says how he'd like to tinker with an old classic hot rod someday. I have a suitcase already packed for my quick escape. He also has the incredible audacity to say how he remembers when I used to help him and that he misses me out there working with him. Hello? I remind him about the swearing and he says it's not so bad. Well I guess I could either learn to ignore the swearing by using ear plugs or I could join him. I think the neighbors would start picketing our house. Maybe, after they call 911 first.

Most people who know my husband would be terribly shocked at how I'm portraying him and would believe that I am making this all up. To most people he is shy and quiet, very polite and considerate. And, most of the time, he is also that way with me. He's truly a good person and that's why I married him. I guess he either feels very comfortable being himself with me or maybe I bring out the worst in him. It could go either way. If ask him about this, he would say "Huh?"

My husband is very active and physical in bed. Yikes! I bet that caught your attention. I mean to say he's a very active sleeper. What's up with the snoring and then not snoring and then not breathing? And then louder snoring? I totally understand the symptoms of sleep apnea, but he needs to see a doctor for that. That's another story, the story about trying to get a husband to go see a doctor about anything.

If his snoring was on an even keel all night long I could sleep through this. In fact it would probably even lull me to sleep. Oh how wonderful that would be! He starts out snoring—he literally falls asleep as soon as his head hits that pillow. He's snoring in two minutes. I mean we'll go to bed together and I could be reaching over the alarm clock to set it for morning, turn off the lamp and roll over to say goodnight to him. Snore. It's that fast. He's so romantic. I used to just let him sleep and I'll roll over disgusted, maybe a little frustrated. I'm not so nice anymore. I'll do things to him like pinch his nostrils closed or elbow him or just jump up and down on the bed. You know it's really funny to see him sit up and wonder where he is and what's going on. I can really be nasty sometimes. I know, sometimes marriage really sucks for him too.

Sometimes I'll be having a bad dream. I'm running and someone or something is chasing me. I can't see it but I know it's there behind me. I can't let it catch me. But no matter how fast I run and duck and jump, it's still right behind me. It's closing the gap. It's closer now. I feel the hot breath on my back and it's growling. It's growling louder and I know it'll catch me soon. I'm sweating and I panic. Growl. Snore. Snore? I realize I'm awake and in bed and my husband is snoring on my back. Wake up! He makes me so mad.

Sometimes my husband will have a bad dream. I'll be sleeping and I can feel the bed jerk and it wakes me up. He's whimpering and his legs are moving like he's running. I must be very careful waking him from this. The last time I just reached out gently to shake him awake he flailed his arms and punched me in the face. He was very apologetic about it and I know it wasn't done on purpose but my nose hurt and I couldn't get back to sleep for a while. It's not something I'm going to forget anytime soon.

The newest thing that my husband does in bed is twitch his feet. I believe he may have restless leg syndrome. I admit that I go to bed with cold feet, I have circulation problems. He'll warm up my feet with his which is a very wonderful thing he does. But as soon as he's sleeping, he kicks me. Just as I'm dozing off! And I need to keep his toenails short because he'll scratch me with his talons. So really, sometimes sleeping in the same bed really sucks.

But my husband really tries to be a good husband. He used to forget our anniversary in the first few years of our marriage. I realize that I may have been a little harsh with him about that. I came to this realization last summer. The License plate tabs on our car was supposed to be renewed in July. For some reason, even knowing this and even having the money and time to get the tabs does not stop us from always procrastinating and using the ten day grace period into August, an interesting thing for a cop. One morning on the day of August 6th I was writing out checks for our monthly bills and found the reminder slip for tab renewal to my husband's car in with the bills. So I panicked (because we had procrastinated again) and I quickly called him. When he answered all I said was "Do you know what day this is?" He said "No, what?" I said "It's August 6th!" There was silence for a moment. He said "Oh honey, I'm sorry. Happy Anniversary!" Our anniversary was still a month away. Now the silence is on my end. You have to hand it to him. He was trying to keep all his bases covered. I told him that he watched too much "Home Improvement" reruns. It was a good try. We did get our tabs in time though, well, before the tenth of the month anyway.

I also learned the hard way to never say that it's okay when my husband forgets my birthday. It used to be that he would remember the day and would write me a homemade card or letter or even buy me a card later that same week. Then he would go with me shopping for a gift and tell me to get whatever. I remember the year we got a new Hyundai Santa Fe in August, seven days before my birthday. Even though we had planned on a new vehicle anyway, I made a comment that it was a great birthday gift. Well that year I got no card, no letter, and no shopping for a gift. I'll never say that again. Unless he buys me another new vehicle next year that's only MY personal vehicle with a sunroof, leather, heated seats and a temperature controlled thermostat interior. With a GPS and hands-free parallel parking. And a 6 disc changer plus auxiliary for my IPhone/IPod. And a built in hands-free blue tooth and 360 video monitor on dashboard for driving in reverse. And 4-wheel drive. I know I can think of more things for it to have, just give me time.

And while we're on the topic of shopping, you know how men are so very bad about asking for directions when driving somewhere and they're lost? My husband goes a step further than this. This also applies to shopping with my husband at a store I'm unfamiliar with. He usually trusts me to find whatever is needed at a retail discount store, after all I've worked in five different stores and they are all very similar. But if he's looking for something on sale at Menard's or Home Depot I'm lost. Not only do I not know *where* to look but nine times out of ten I don't even know *what* he's looking for. Do you think he'll ask a clerk or associate who works there? Nope. He'll circle the store several times and call it every name he can think of and pass by a dozen employees. I'll finally throw my hands up and drag a clerk over to him. I can't explain what we're looking for; I don't know what it is. The poor clerk is probably wondering why we're so hostile towards him and why he's been taken hostage. Especially when the product we're looking for is always only one or two aisles away and we've already walked by it four times.

My husband also doesn't understand the concept of the use of instructions in assembling furniture or etc. One example is a futon sofa. We bought two of them and he was to assemble them downstairs in the family room. Looks easy enough but why so many screws? After a couple of hours and yes, a lot of swearing, he decided to use the sheet of paper with pictures on it called "the instructions". He completed the project smoothly afterwards, using every screw. You would think he could learn from this. And yet . . . no.

Men are so confusing and often funny just by their actions. When we were younger, we went regularly to the racquet and fitness club. We loved to play racquetball and became quite proficient being very competitive. We were smart enough to play for the exercise and not to keep points. That would always lead to fighting. We did however follow all the rules and could always tell who was having a good day by the number of times that person served. So why does he run circles around me and make whooping noises like Curly from the three stooges just when I'm in the groove and serious about the game? Then he gets hit hard by the ball in the middle of his back while screwing around. And I'm supposed to feel sorry for him. Well I did laugh at him a lot. After all, he was asking to get hit.

It's true that we are very competitive. It's how we met. In college we were together in the Army R.O.T.C.—that's short for Reserve Officer Training Corps—and we did a lot of extra-curricular army-type activities together. Things like the color guard, ranger challenge, field training exercises, cadet corps night, the army kept us busy besides our trying to keep up our full time classes with decent grades. I had a 2 1/2 year scholarship and he transferred from the regular army. We both had a contract to fulfill so were in for the long haul. And we were young and had a lot to prove. Yet I could always keep a few points ahead of him. I was commander of the color guard. I was the cadet sergeant major in our junior year (highest attainable rank) and the cadet battalion commander in our senior year (again highest attainable rank, blush). He was good about it and never held a grudge against me—we were the best of friends. That's where it ends. In any sport like tennis, racquetball, monopoly, he's ruthless. And then there's a lot of fighting. And yelling. So the best thing we ever did was to decide not to keep score. We still know who's ahead by the one who's always serving. We still play by the rules.

Monopoly on the other hand is never played in our house. He's an evil mastermind and wants complete world domination even if it means making a 10 year old cry. Now there's a memory. It was at his parent's house and we were playing Monopoly with his niece and nephew, the summer before we were married. He won the game by taking over and "monopolizing" everybody very ruthlessly. His nephew was hurt and confused by the game. I gave him my property and some of my money to help his feelings—I was practicing to be a good parent after all. The man was a brute! And yet I still married the ruthless man. Maybe I'm the confusing one.

Through all his faults and just plain silliness and weirdness, I love him very much and the following chapters will just give a little insight of how we've managed to stay married to each other for these 26 years and how I can't imagine a life without him, through thick or thin . . . yes, I said thick, we've both gained weight . . .

Chapter Two

Define "Happily Married"

So what, then, is a happy marriage? Do you really expect to be smiling for the rest of your life because you married the man of your dreams (or a close runner-up)? Let's face it—it's not in human nature to be happy all of the time. Or to feel good all of the time. Or even to feel content all of the time. It's because Adam and Eve ate that forbidden fruit and now we all have these imperfections like greed, envy, jealousy, spite, sloth, etc. Everyone should expect to have days when you're not happy, when you don't want to get along with people, when you're feeling selfish, when you want something more out of life, when you're feeling just plain bitchy.

Reality is that no one can actually have a wonderfully perfectly "happy" marriage. You can have "happy" days. You can have a "good" marriage. You can have a "strong" marriage. And this is what my husband and I have worked hard to achieve. It's not perfect, it's just good and it's strong.

Our good marriage needs to be built upon like a house, don't laugh. We married each other because we were in love. So we had this love to build on like a foundation. We had our first fight and we were both heartbroken, even felt disillusioned. We felt things were falling apart. Then we made up and we learned something new about each other. Not only did we patch the crumbling mortar but we reinforced our house and now it has become stronger.

Let's say you're "happily complacent". Can you just imagine how boring that would be? To always agree with each other, to never raise your voice, to never have any excitement? How would you handle any real emotions? What is up with these couples who say they never fight? To me it sounds like a lot of suppressed anger and frustration. Or maybe just plain boring and without real passion? I think a good fight is healthy—once in a while. Maybe not a physical one with a lot of name-calling, especially in front of the kids, that's never good. But a good disagreement or heated argument can definitely

20

spice up your marriage. And maybe you'll learn something more about each other. I really believe in the old saying that there is a fine line between love and hate. It's all included in passion and if you're passionate about someone or something, you feel the whole range of human emotions, good and bad. (Please keep in mind that this is my book, and it is just my opinion—I am not an analyst.)

How devastated would you be after several years of complacency to actually come to a disagreement and argue? After years of complacency, you finally put your marriage to the test by a good strong disagreement. Would this now lead to instant divorce and "disillusionment of marriage"? Sometimes the best ideas/solutions are the products of a good disagreement. So come on! Throw a shoe at him once in a while! He'll learn to duck. And this may actually save your marriage. Who knows? Isn't it worth a try? And it feels really good.

Yes, my husband and I do fight and it's not always one sided. Sometimes it is **just** him and sometimes (I admit it) it is **just** me. But most of the time it's a little of the both of us. The good thing about our marriage is that we can talk about it afterwards. The tough part is that I want to talk immediately afterwards because I'm over it that fast. My husband, on the other hand, needs a couple of days to cool off. By that time I'm mad all over again. He says I don't respect his need for time to reflect and settle down. I say he doesn't respect my need for immediate resolution and closure. After about 10 years of this, I finally bit down and tried to wait for him. At the same time he tried a day sooner. We still fight but now we're over it quicker. It gives us an extra day to fight about something else. We do try to save when we can. Nobody's perfect.

We also learned that talking is not good enough. We now take turns listening to each other. That's very hard to do. I'm a really good talker but when I'm upset or when he's not making any sense to me, I don't listen really well. I always thought he was a better listener than me so then why is it that his hearing is so bad? He looks like he's listening but he doesn't get a word I say. I know we're both speaking the same language, aren't we? I may say something like "You need to stop being so hard on your son. He's a good kid and is trying very hard to please you." He's hearing "I think you're stupid and I love my son more than you." I know he loves our son and is very proud of him. But our son is a lot like me in his thinking and so I can understand him better. It makes my husband confused and feeling left out. It took me a long time to figure this one out. We're still working on it. But I wish he'd listen to what I mean as well as to what I say. Life would be so much easier if I could just hit him over the head with something and he would suddenly understand what I was saying to him, like in cave-man days. Or maybe if I could push an "easy" button like on those office supply store commercials. Then he would say "yes dear" to everything. Oh right, and then we would be back to dullsville. What can you do? Maybe I could have a Stepford husband. Why hasn't someone made **that** movie?

A lot of us go into marriage expecting to be like our parents. Or possibly some would like a marriage opposite of one like their parents. Nonetheless, we all want a marriage that is perfect, that will stand the test of time. I grew up wanting a good marriage full of love and respect and caring like my parents have. I wanted a man like my dad: tall, dark, handsome, popular, charming, intelligent, dependable, and would take care of everything. Even though I knew that I was nothing like my mom: small, pretty, gentle, patient, giving 110% of herself to her family—my mom is Japanese and very traditional in her role as mother to her family. She's the perfect mom. I, on the other hand, am tall, compassionate though not too gentle, impatient, and I try to give 110% to my husband and children when I'm not being ornery or stubborn. I am still old-fashioned in a modern kind of way.

I found a man similar to my dad in all but looks and personality. My husband is handsome but not tall and dark; he is average height and fair. He is very intelligent, dependable and can be charming when he chooses to be. But I found out the hard way that he cannot take care of everything and that I was going to have to do my part. In my family my dad took care of all the bills, balancing the bank account, contacting utilities/repairmen etc. In my husband's family, his mother took care of all this. He expected me to do everything and I expected that of him. I won and he was in charge of the household accounts. He failed. He just didn't keep track of bills, didn't like to make phone calls, he was just too big of a procrastinator to keep up. I took over and have kept track ever since. Not that I'm the greatest with a budget but I'm passable. He just works hard and hands the paychecks over to me and trusts me to take care of everything. That's really a lot of trust when you think about it. Actually, now that I think about it, maybe he won after all. He doesn't have to balance a budget now, I took over that headache. Darn it, he's more intelligent than I thought!

My husband's personality is very different from my dad's but that's actually a good thing since my personality is very similar to my dad's. I'm short tempered but recover quickly. I am very outgoing and make friends easily. I'm quite bossy and am not afraid to try new things. I may be hot tempered but never hold a grudge. I'm slightly impulsive and don't always take the time to look at things from all angles. My husband is a careful man. He never makes a quick decision but weighs all possibilities. He's even tempered but when angry, will hold on to his anger for days. He's a bit shy but if you get to know him, he becomes a loyal friend. He has a laid back nature but can hold a grudge until the next ice age. And he's constant—doesn't feel the need to always try new things. If it's not broke, why fix it—if it works, why change?

He's had the same job for 23 years and plans another 10 until retirement. He and my dad are both very good men and I fight with both of them. Doesn't mean I don't love them.

Things have changed a lot for us in the last few years. I decided to try a salaried management position in my job at a major retail store. The decision was not made lightly. The family—my husband, myself and our three children whose ages at that time were 7, 11 and 15—sat at the dining room table and discussed this decision. It would mean a lot more support from the rest of the family to help mom with household duties. Chores such as vacuuming, daily dishes, laundry, taking care of the dog and even cooking supper was going to be shared by all of us now, not just mom. The kids all made faces (except for my seven year old who thought this would be fun because she thinks everything is fun and is very impulsive because she's seven!) but we explained the extra income would help pay for college and stuff (yeah, like that really happened) and then they were all right with it. You know, I don't really know why we have these family discussions except to say that we had a family discussion over something. My husband and I can usually talk the kids into or out of something because we are very logical (and manipulative) and when we go over how they can help, it lasts for maybe a day. Everyone still asks me what's for supper, I still have to make sure the dog gets fed, laundry is up for grabs—sometimes it's me sometimes it's dad, I have to yell at my teenage daughter daily to do the dishes, the vacuuming just doesn't happen. And let's not discuss the bathrooms.

I've worked a third shift job now for 13 out of the last 15 years and have had to sleep during the day when I can. With an eight hour a day job, this is not a problem. I could still sleep six to eight hours and spend time doing household chores and running errands on days I work. Now I work 13 to 14 hours a day and am lucky to get four hours of sleep. I'm tired and crabby most days and could care less about my messy house or what's for dinner. The daily stress of dealing with childish customers and childish employees makes me even crabbier and less patient with my childish children and husband. And the stories I could tell about the silly, crazy, and slightly dangerous things people do at my store could fill another book. I constantly have to remind myself that I'm working this job for my family, that it's just a job, to not take it home with me. But when I spend more time there than I do at my own home, it gets hard to remember. And there are several days when I know it's hard for my husband to live with me.

We both have jobs where we deal with people. He's a cop and deals—usually—with the worst of human nature. Well at least he gets to carry a gun and a big stick and can hit people over the head with it when provoked. There are days when I really, really, really wish I had a big stick. But I must remind myself that I am a manager and must always remember that the customer comes first! My husband, as a cop, has the ability to speak to an offender using language that he/she can understand. If every other word is an expletive, than he can speak back to that person in the same way. I really, really, really wish I could speak to those mean, nasty customers in the same language that they use with me. But I must always remember to speak respectfully and that the customer is always first! Please don't get me wrong. Perhaps 90% of our customers are good, kind, honest, hard-working people that just want to get the best prices for their hard-earned money. It's the other 10% that ruin it for everyone, that makes it tougher to return things and are just rip-off artists and thieves. Am I a little bitter? I say no. I'm more than a little. It's sad really.

But enough of that! My husband and I must remember that sometimes we get a little hard on our children and on each other and must back off. He's very good at not using that bad language in front of the kids. I'm not as good though and must watch myself. I think it's because I must watch my language at work and all that suppression must have somewhere to go. And I must quit using the word "must" so much.

Sometimes my husband and I will go through a long stretch of fighting every week for a month or two and we wonder if we're really happily married at all? I think back and remember some good years of not fighting much at all and some rough years when we fought a lot. We seem to go through cycles of testing each other. But I think we always weigh the odds. I mean, we always imagine how we would be without each other and it's not an option. Even when I'm so very angry at him and say mean things to him to hurt him, I know even while yelling at him that I don't really mean it. I'm the one that says the hurtful things to get a response. That's me—thinking any response is better than none. It doesn't matter who started the fight. I'm the yeller and he has only learned to become a yeller in the last 10 years of our marriage. But we always know it'll pass and we make up because we must. We belong together, we fit together and we love each other. We must be patient with each other—I really struggle with that, it's true, because I'm the emotional one. But true happiness in our marriage is in knowing that he loves me even with all my faults and I love him with all of his faults too. It's respecting each other **and** loving each other—both are what have kept us together for more than 20 years.

Chapter Three

Three Simple Words

Why do husbands think wives are so hard to understand? The majority of wives just want appreciation, love and respect. We just want to be listened to and if we're upset and there's an argument or a fight, all it takes to get us back is to say "I love you" and "I'll try to understand". But most especially those first three words. It really works. It's really all we need and everything's good again. Why is this so complicated for husbands? We can even spell it out for you and yet you'll still argue with us that you don't know what we want to hear. If the husband really feels love for his wife, he should work on saying it. I know some men can't phrase those three words together very well, but they should really try if they want to work some magic. It really works miracles after a fight. Because wives are always thinking "you don't really love me". See we're not that complicated. It's really quite simple. Why are men so stubborn?

If the wife leaves upset and the husband wants her back, don't ever say "just come home and we'll talk". That will never work. She'll never come back to that. What she wants to hear is "I love you and I **wish** you would come back so that we can talk". It may mean the same thing to a husband but it means so much more to a wife. And if the wife leaves the house upset and needs time to herself, don't call her to get her back home and then ask what's for supper? What is up with that? If you want a response that doesn't involve getting seriously injured, you'd better offer to cook it yourself or to take her out to eat. Taking your wife out to eat is always a great idea. I can't count how many times my husband has fought me over that. If he would bring it up more often, he would win more fights later because I would let him, thinking that I owe him one or two since he took me out to eat. It's really very simple.

My husband once told me during a fight that he thought that I kept score on things. I remember telling him that was a terrible thing to say because I don't keep score. But when thinking about how we do things, like in the last example of going out to eat, maybe I do keep some kind of score. I could possibly be doing this subconsciously, not really intending to do so. He really is smarter than I thought!

Actually I married a man that was very smart. I could never marry a man that I thought was less intelligent than me. In college, when we met, we would both be in the same class and I would cram for my test in order to get a good grade. I was a high achiever and needed A's besides my being a scholarship student. My husband could read something once, then walk into a test cold and ace it. Even without studying. How sick is that? And without cramming he could always manage to retain this knowledge. I crammed, maybe I would ace the test, and then weeks later couldn't tell you any of the answers. Well some, maybe. But I solidly admit that cramming is not a great way to learn.

My husband says he uses logic and common sense to find his answers. He is very street smart. But in order to use logic, you must have some knowledge to back it up. We all know too many people who will out right argue their case based on their understanding of logic and common sense that sound like complete idiots when they talk. I can mention a few politicians who do this.

So my husband will often argue with me that he doesn't think he is smarter than me, that he thinks I am much smarter than he is. It took me over 10 years to understand retail management. I can explain several merchandising, operational and financial aspects of running a successful retail business establishment to him. He says he doesn't understand retail. But after I tell him something once, he retains it. The only things I remember about law enforcement are the funny stories he tells me about people he deals with on the street daily while performing his job. I could never remember the city ordinances or state and county laws that he must retain in his memory, even when he tells me about them repeatedly. Maybe because I don't have to, but still, it's harder for me.

But my husband is not completely dense about our relationship. I know he says he thinks I'm smarter than him mainly because then he will stay on my good side and not get in trouble. He could possibly believe it, I don't really know. We do make a good team. The things I don't understand, he does and vice-versa. So why do we keep fighting so much?

I believe it comes down to this: all lasting relationships, the ones where there is no cheating (affairs) and no separations for long periods of time (business or military possibly) are because we have a love/hate relationship. It's not really "hate"; it's actually "hurt". If you love someone so much that you know you can't exist without them, that they are truly your other half, then when misunderstandings happen it hurts so bad that you want to hurt them back equally. You lash back hence the fighting.

Let's clarify the word "fighting". I'm not talking about slapping and hitting and being physical. I'm talking about fighting with words and feelings. It's more than arguing; it's intended to cause hurt and confusion. Its emotions brought out in words that can hurt just as much as a physical blow. My husband is a good man and would never physically harm me, not that he could without getting hurt in return. I am a strong and large woman. I'm almost the same height and only about 30 pounds less weight than my husband. I can hold my own in a physical fight, though my emotions may get in the way. But his words have always had the power to knock me out cold. But I know my own mouth; I know I've probably hurt him more times than he has hurt me. There I go keeping score again.

It never matters what the subject of a fight is, I can never remember our petty reasons for our fights afterwards and neither can he. The fight may be about money, the kids, money, the in-laws, money . . . anyway, the reason doesn't matter. It can always end peacefully and quickly if one of says the magic phrase. I tried it one day, on vacation this last year in New England. My husband was angry about always driving (his idea, I kept asking if I could drive but he kept refusing) and how tired he was and how expensive things were and how he wished he never came. I remembered this chapter I was writing and how I felt when we fought. So I just asked him, with tears in my eyes, "but I love you. Don't you still love me?" And just like that, he softened and said "yes, of course I love you. That will never change." And our fight was over with lots of hugs and kisses. Then we changed our sight-seeing plans and pushed them back so he could have one day of just napping and reading a book and being lazy. So the three simple words are a lesson for wives as well as husbands. Wives just probably need to hear them more often. Husbands, please remember this.

Those three simple words never get old. In this age of information and technology, we communicate by text message some days more than talking. I can look at the history of our texts over that last year and can find countless "I love you baby" messages from him. It certainly helps when we can't see each other as much as we would like. Even after 26 years, when he speaks or writes those three words, it still creates a warm fuzzy feeling inside me. So no, the words "I love you" never lose their meaning and can never be over used.

There are times when "I love you" doesn't seem to be enough. It is during those moments when I think about how lucky I am compared to so many people I know that either do not have a good marriage or still haven't found their match that I wonder if those three words really say enough. I remind myself that it's not the three words that aren't enough. It's just talking and communicating and reminding my husband about all the good things that we have that are so wonderful and how lucky we are that we even found each other that make up the difference. This extra communication backs up those three words and makes them stronger. Nothing is stronger than love. And no phrase is stronger than "I love you".

Chapter Four

Raising Our Kids

One could call us strict parents. We have always had very set rules and routines for our three children. This is something the both of us have always agreed on. It is how we were raised and we greatly respect our parents because of it. However, it is not easy to do.

Our first child happened unexpectedly and though we were completely unprepared and very young, he was, and still is, a great blessing, like all of our children.

My husband and I were married on September 6, 1986. Douglas James, our happy, bouncing (literally, he could never stay still) baby boy was born February 6, 1987. We never called him Douglas. He was called Digger, a nickname he had since the womb. Don't ask why, we just came up with that name. And he was the cutest and best behaved baby we could have asked for—the perfect first child.

Digger was the perfect baby. However, he had some health issues. He was born 3 weeks early in the winter, so he had some jaundice and I had to bring him in to the hospital weekly for a bilirubin check and keep him in the sun as much as possible. At five months, he had an intussusception; his intestines telescoped into each other and made a blockage so nothing could flow through. Apparently we were lucky. Hard to say while waiting in emergency as doctors cut my baby open but because his tissues were not damaged and we had caught it soon enough, they only needed to pull the intestines straight and no cutting and stitching together of the intestine was necessary. Only the scar remains under his belly button today. Still my baby son was hooked up to tubes in a lonely crib in the hospital and I couldn't hold him. He was just starting to crawl and wanted to move around. He couldn't understand that I could not take him out of the crib and hold him. He whimpered and cried a lot—this was very unlike my happy healthy child.

The hospital staff gave me a cot in his room so I could stay with him. Okay folks; just try to make me leave. That event would have made the 6 o'clock news. He recovered quickly, though at the time it seemed like forever. Babies and children bounce back so quickly. I think it's because they don't dwell on how rotten they feel and feel sorry for themselves like adults do. They just want to feel better so they can go and play. After healing quickly from the intussusception, Digger stayed a very healthy child.

I remember when Digger was barely 2 years old and we were driving to visit my parents. They lived three hours away. Digger was in the back seat strapped into his car seat. At two years old he could barely make a full sentence, though he was an early achiever and spoke clearly. I had given him a cookie and he was messy, crumbs everywhere. My husband made a fuss about how messy Digger was, getting crumbs all over the car. There was silence then a small voice from the back seat said "I just a baby . . ." I guess my two year old had heard me say that on several occasions so he just repeated what he had heard before. It was worth a good laugh at the time. But little did we know there was a lesson to be learned from this.

Later, in the same year, when Digger was still 2 years old, he was getting strapped into his car seat in our old pickup truck, an old Ford F150. Daddy was trying very hard not to swear, it was always difficult to hook up to the bench seat's existing seat belts. As Daddy was tugging and pulling at the straps and not getting it to work, Digger, looking down at daddy, said "somovabich . . ." He had good little ears back then and we learned our first lesson as parents. Watch what you say in front of the little ones because they are like parrots. Just repeating what they hear.

I remember Digger having a difficult time relating to children of his own age. He spoke clearly and at three years of age, he spoke full sentences and some interesting phrases. I remember that Christmas when he was three years old, when he told everyone he was "independent" because he had been watching Rudolph the Red Nosed Reindeer and that is what Rudolph said. During the summer when he was three and a half, I was with him in the city playground and a nearby church had let their summer bible school children out to play. The kindergarten age children all ran and milled around Digger and he was so happy that he started hopping up and down and running in circles. Now other three year olds may just join in and run in circles too. But not big five and six year olds. They thought Digger was definitely special needs, so they quietly left and played on their own. Digger didn't care and continued climbing and playing like he was doing before they came. Digger was also very tall for his age and so this added to the older children's confusion, he was taller than most of them.

Digger stayed very healthy after the very real scare of his intussusception, but we had yet to experience child number two.

Pamela Jo was born 3 ½ years after her big brother. We called her Jo-Jo, a nickname she still has today (actually I think I'm the only one who still calls her that, or just Jo for short). Jo-Jo was a beautiful baby girl, how lucky were we to have a boy and a girl! I was on bed rest for almost 2 months with some pre-term labor but she was born a very healthy 8 pound baby. She immediately fell in love with her big brother and must, at all costs, keep up with him and/or beat him at everything! Therefore my accident-prone child was created.

When Jo-Jo was barely 2 years old, she was playing with her big brother (who was 5) in the living room. Digger was holding her by both arms and twirling her around in a circle. He let go and she fell backwards, on her elbows. I only know this because this is what Digger told me they were doing. I was not watching at that moment, being only steps away in the kitchen. Anyway, she cried and I held her. She held her head funny and I was very worried so I took her to the emergency room, afraid of a concussion or something that was wrong.

After asking me all kinds of questions regarding child abuse,(nice, I know it's their job but still . . .) they took x-rays and after someone calling themselves a physician looked her over, declared she was fine and just needed some Tylenol for whip-lash. So I took her home, believing the fool. She cried through the night and the next morning, she could not lift her head. Furious, I called the hospital and they apologized, oh we missed a crack on her clavicle (collar bone), yes I had to take her back in to be fitted for a brace. Charlatans!

A year later, when Jo-Jo was 3 years old, she was playing in the rumpus room in the basement with her brother and tripped over some toys or something. Again, I had to take her brother's word for it since I was not watching, having the need to tell the same story to the staff in the emergency room. This time, Jo bit her bottom lip almost completely off, held on by just the skin. I got a cool damp cloth and held it to her mouth holding her lip together. They stitched it back together in the ER. Today, if she smiles or laughs you can see a half moon shaped line on her bottom lip but thankfully it is not obvious. Again I received a barrage of questions regarding child abuse.

Another year later, when Jo-Jo was 4 years old, she was playing in the bedroom with her brother, again, and she tripped over the fan on the floor. Her bottom teeth went through the flesh below her bottom lip. This required stitches inside and outside her mouth. I think they quit asking me child abuse questions now because they were not seeing any other signs of abuse, maybe they were finally believing that Jo was just a klutz.

Six months later, when Jo-Jo was 4 ½ years old, she was playing at Bachan and Jichan's house (Grandma and Grandpa in Japanese), and she ran into the door latch being just the right height and punched a hole in her forehead.

Being in another city, I received the usual child abuse questions and she received some more stitches. Oh and the best is yet to come.

We made it almost 3 more years before any other major catastrophes that a Band-Aid couldn't handle. When Jo-Jo was 7 years old, she was trying to keep up with the older boys in the backyard on the big swing set. Jon, a big third grader, was swinging high then jumping off and running with his legs in the air before landing on the ground. Thank god nothing happened to him. Jo-Jo, of course not to be out-done by a mere boy, had to do the same stunt. She swung high, jumped off, changed her mind, and landed on her wrists. She snapped her right wrist so bad it was mangled.

I had a houseful of ladies, having a candle party at the time, the reason why so many kids were in the back yard. All I remember were women screaming, some were crying, and I was trying to make sure Jo-Jo would remain calm. Bringing her to the emergency room this time, I remember this as a time they did not make her wait in the lobby at all. Her mangled arm was scary to look at (it was broken and looked like the letter "z", really). I remember they gave her something, maybe morphine, and she felt so much better, that while her father and I were asked to leave the room so they could set her arm, she waved at us. I remember her doctor saying, "no honey, not with that arm . . ."

Not finished yet, when we returned to her room after they set her arm, she was crying again. The doctor asked her where it hurt, was it the arm still? She said her shoulder hurt. More x-rays later and she had also broken her clavicle. Again. Really Jo? But with her arm already in a sling to hold her wrist in place, they did not suggest a brace. She was given pain meds and told to TRY not to run around for a while. Good luck with that advice. Her arm healed quickly, even though it was the end of the school year and she missed a lot of summer not getting wet. Sometimes parenting really sucks!

She had one more trip to the emergency room as a child one year later when she was eight. Again on the swing set in the back yard with a yard full of children. If my memory serves me correctly, there was always a back yard full of children. Anyway, she spun around and around on the swing and then let loose, spinning wildly. She spun and hit her head on the heavy wooden railroad tie legs of the swing set and got a concussion (discovering this later). She came into the house crying. I gave her Tylenol and told her to lie down. She came out of her room and told me she was going to throw up, which she did. Then she fell down, her legs felt funny. Then she talked gibberish, like her tongue was too big or something. Having read about concussions, I took her again to the emergency room. This time the triage nurse looked at her and said she's just sick, yelled at her when she threw up in the waiting room, and six hours later, when Jo finally got to see another nurse, they said she was fine. Six hours later! Of course she was fine, I made sure she was fine, or else she would have been dead! Thank goodness my daughter has a hard head. To this day I don't know what damage she may have incurred but I certainly hope and pray that nothing happens to her later in life because of this stupid hospital's emergency center. Really, all it takes is one stupid nurse who has no business being in the field of medicine to ruin any of the good that all the others do every day. Still a little bitter about that day, I am.

Jo-Jo grew some more and refrained from any more trips to the emergency room, that I can remember. I'm exhausted with just the memories of those trips to the hospital. Now I'm exhausted just writing about them.

Baby number three was born when Digger, now Doug because he was a big boy now and was embarrassed by the nickname Digger so could we just call him Doug, was 8 years old and Jo-Jo was 4 ½ years old. We had another baby girl, and we named her Sarah Jean. There was no shortening of her name, didn't want to call her by her middle name like we did with Jo, so we called her Peanut.

Peanut was a beautiful platinum blond, peaches and cream complexion, light blue eyed, perfect and petite baby girl. Looked nothing like me. I remember bringing her to the clinic for her well-child visits and the doctor asked me why the child care provider was bringing her in for her appointment and not her mother? What? It's my baby and I'm the momma! The doctor was Hispanic and had a dark complexion similar to myself and she assumed I was either Hispanic or Native American. I get that a lot. No one guesses I'm half Asian. Anyway, Sarah had a complexion like her father, who is Swedish, Finnish, and Czech. Her father also was a platinum blond as a child. Actually, all my children have blue eyes like their father; I'm the only one in this family with brown eyes. Something about a recessive gene and my father is blue-eyed but my mother is brown eyed and no one in her family has blue eyes, of course, being Japanese. So none of my three sisters or I could have ever had blue eyes. Ken's family is all blue-eyed. Therefore my children all inherited blue eyes from my father and their father. Okay, enough on the lesson in genetics. It's the only thing I know and I hope I got it right. My husband is the biologist in the family, I never took the class. I couldn't cut up a frog, much less a baby pig.

Peanut got the benefit of having a brother old enough to help babysit and a sister who also helped (when she felt like it). However, sadly to say, she told me one day when she was ten that she was sad that we never had another baby after her. Because "Doug got Pam and I got nobody". It made me very sad because I had my tubes tied after Sarah was born since I was again on bed rest with pre-term labor and the doctor suggested permanent sterilization. It saddens me to this day because I always wanted four children just so this wouldn't happen. It's good to have an even count, so that there isn't a third child out, so to say. I reminded Sarah how special it is to be the baby and that she got all of our attention and didn't have to share Mom and Dad with another baby. It didn't help.

Sarah was a very happy and well-adjusted baby. Another very easy baby to raise. But she didn't receive as much attention from Mom as the other two did as small children. When Sarah was two, I decided I wanted to get back into the work force. Except for my years in the National Guard, which was only one weekend a month and two weeks out of the summer, I only did some odd jobs here and there. I worked for a couple months at a grocery store, and then a couple months for a department store but I kept getting pregnant and didn't want to work with a newborn so I kept leaving my employment.

But since I was having no more babies and Sarah was out of diapers and off the formula, I wanted to work. So I went to work for a major retailer, working graveyard shift so I could get home early in the morning so my husband could go to work and we would require no day care provider. This was important to me. I wanted complete control on how my children were raised, even though I realize there are some good day care providers out there and have nothing bad to say about them and the mothers who must use them. This was just my choice.

So I worked overnight hours and came home in the morning, slept an hour, got my two older children off to school, spent the morning with my two year old Peanut, and lay down to nap when I could. I slept again in the evening for an hour or two when my husband came home from work.

I remember one day, I was tired of the couch and Sarah was down for her nap so I thought I could sneak an hour or two nap on my bed. Leaving the door open so I could hear, I'm a very light sleeper; I went to my room and slept on the bed. It makes me crazy just thinking about that now, anything could have happened to a two year old in that time! But I remember waking up suddenly because I sensed something was wrong. The house was too quiet, the TV was off. I know I left it on for background noise for Peanut. I jumped up and swung my legs to the side of the bed and stepped down to the squishy floor. The floor shouldn't have been squishy. I stepped on Peanut, who was sleeping on the floor between my bed and the dresser. She had laid her blankie on the floor and a pillow and had her Pooh Bear with her and was sleeping next to my bed. Thank goodness I didn't put all my weight on my legs yet. After that day, Peanut took her naps on my bed with me. She was such a good little girl and very quiet. Too quiet. She also was the one who turned the TV off because mommy wasn't in the living room. Such a good little girl!

My three beautiful children all grew up into beautiful adults. Sarah my baby, who I can't call Peanut anymore, is a senior and is graduating this year. My two older children, Doug (25) and Pamela Jo (22) both have full time jobs but haven't been able to afford to move out yet. It makes me happy and sad at the same time. I am blessed to still have all my children under one roof.

However, the other side is that they are grown up adults and should have a place of their own. One is having problems finding a house that he and his friends can afford and the other is having problems finding roommates to move out with. They do not want to live together, most of the time the two oldest can barely tolerate each other. They tried college, didn't like it, but are still thinking of going back to school. In the meantime, they are very good at their jobs.

Sarah has plans for college in the fall. She is the one with the great grades, honor society, debate team, very organized, her future mapped out. She will have a good husband and lots of children. She will never live far away from Mom and Dad because she will miss us too much. And she needs to have Mom's good cooking very close for herself and my grandchildren (actually all three children have said that—yay for me!). And she needs to have Dad fix things for her. Like I said, she has things very planned. Jo just goes day to day and if the guy is hot, she may go out with him or not, but she is saving herself for Adam Levine (Maroon 5). Doug is too busy running around with his friends and will not be serious about any one relationship. He is my laid-back, take things as they come, will do anything for his friends, hey there's only one of me, kind of guy. And he will do anything for his baby sister Sarah Peanut which has been very helpful in her teenage years without a sibling to share school things with. Yes, Doug has been like a third parent to Sarah, a very hot, hip, all her friends are drooling over him, kind of parent. Doug would have been a hippy if this was the 60's but instead he is a poster ad for American Eagle, the Gap or Urban Outfitters. He'll kill me if he knew I included the word hippy and himself in the same sentence.

Our children are good people and my goal in raising them has been to raise them like my parents raised me and my sisters. We will be there for them but we will not make all their decisions for them. It is very difficult to not want to be in their daily business, to let go of our children, even if they live under your roof. It is very difficult to treat our children like they are adults, like they are real people. I just want them to remain children and listen to mom! Sometimes letting go really sucks!

I cannot have a chapter on raising our children without mentioning our family dog, Fancy. Fancy came to us unexpectedly when Sarah was only two years old. Fancy was one of five puppies belonging to our neighbors across the street. They had a registered Springer Spaniel. Their Spaniel got together with a Golden Retriever. So Fancy was a mixed breed, a pretty black puppy with a white spot on her collar onto her breast and a white tip of her tail. Otherwise she was all black and had the look of both breeds of dogs. We were not looking for a dog; we were given the puppy as a thank you for helping our neighbors one day. She was a very quiet puppy, only two months old and only crying a little on her first night with us, away from her mother and the other pups. I laid on the floor in the dining room with her where we had set up a kennel and bed for her on that first night. The next night we set her kennel next to my side of the bed in our bedroom. That's when I became Mom to her.

I've never known a smarter dog. If we told her no, she remembered and didn't do it. But she would look so sad. She loved all children and loved to play in the fenced yard with all our kids and the neighborhood children every day. She loved to go down the slide and tried very hard to go on the swings with the kids too. If I took the kids to the playground at the city park, Fancy went on the playground too. We went to the Vet regularly for shots or when she was sick. When she was three months old, she had "puppy strangles". Her lymph glands were swollen and if not treated, she would not be able to breathe. So Fancy was referred to the University Veterinary Hospital and put on steroids for several months and also had ear drops. She came to love cheese—I would wrap her steroid pills in a small piece of American cheese and she loved it. It was a treat for her. All the puppies in her litter contracted this disease. Fancy was the only one to survive it.

I was Mom and my husband, Ken was Dad to her. It's funny how she saw our children. Doug our oldest was like another parent for Fancy and she treated him like another adult though he was only 10 when we got her. Pamela Jo rough-housed and wrestled on the floor with her since Fancy was a puppy so Fancy considered Pamela another dog—her equal. Sarah was only two when we got Fancy and since Fancy matured much faster than Sarah, Fancy treated Sarah like an annoying little puppy and ignored her a lot, much to Sarah's frustration.

Fancy lived to be 12 years old and died October 2009 of internal bleeding from a ruptured tumor. It was very unexpected. We knew Fancy had arthritis and was having difficulty going up and down the stairs. One day she could not get up. My husband, Pamela and I took her to the vet. We were recommended an animal hospital by our usual vet for possible surgery; the vet said she had a tumor and some internal bleeding. The vet at the hospital told us there was a 50% chance of survival if Fancy had surgery but a 99% chance the tumor would grow back in 6 months. We had to make the decision right there to put her down. It was the hardest thing we had ever done. She still tried to wag her tail; she looked hopeful that we were going to bring her home. I couldn't bring her home that day. I will never be able to forgive myself for not bringing her home. I always brought her home from the vet and gave her a treat. I didn't bring her home.

No matter what anyone says about animals being insignificant in God's plan for us, I will never believe it. When an animal is intelligent, gentle, compassionate, and loving, there is a soul in them. All souls go to heaven. That thought is what helps me when I think of Fancy, the reason why I will never have another dog. None can replace her in my house or my heart.

Chapter Five

The 51:49 Ratio

What is the 51:49 Ratio? It is something my mother taught me. My mother and father have been married now for 49 years. They have had many serious trials in their marriage but they are still together. I will talk about them more in the chapter about the in-laws. However, my mother is a very good role model and a very smart woman—especially when it comes to having a great marriage.

The 51:49 Ratio means simply this. Always try to give your husband 51% of everything. The old saying about marriage is that everything is 50/50. This does not work. Someone will always think they are not getting their equal share or that the other is being selfish and this leads to hard feelings. There are enough things in a marriage to fight about. But if you go into a marriage where you want more for your spouse than you want for yourself, then it's a good start.

When my husband and I went for our marriage compatibility test with our pastor, a wonderful, gentle man and a good solid Baptist minister from my small hometown, our test results showed something very interesting. We thought it meant we must know each other's favorite colors or favorite TV shows, that it was a test of knowledge about each other. The compatibility test was not to be a determination of whether or not we knew each other perfectly well or that we would have similar personalities. It was a test of whether or not we understood each other. After taking the test, our Pastor Harold told us that he was impressed that we rated each other's personality the same however I was willing to be more generous with my husband's faults by being less harsh and my husband did the same with mine. Pastor Harold said this was a good thing and very important in a marriage, to be more forgiving of each other's faults than of our own. I really didn't know the significance of this until after being married for several years and I've remembered Pastor's advice even after all this time. The other thing I remember that he told us was to never go to bed angry at each other. Well one out of two isn't bad.

So when my husband and I share a dessert, I make sure he gets the best pieces and the last bite. The best part is that he tries to do the same with me. Some days he wins but I must be careful. Many times when I say "okay, I'll have the last bite", he'll say sadly, "Oh, I thought you'd say no . . ." This example applies to a lot in our marriage.

We've shared the same bed now for 26 years. I always make sure he gets plenty of room on his half. I try not to hog the covers and I make sure I give him more. Of course, if I'm unconscious, all bets are off. Also, if his second pillow (he needs two or else his snoring will be unbearable) is a little over mine, it must be moved immediately. He can have two pillows but I need my one whole pillow.

When we go out to eat as a family to a restaurant, he gets first choice on where to sit. Being a cop, he always has the need to sit with his back to the wall, with a clear view of all entrances and exits. However, it always ends up being a problem, a game of musical chairs with a very confused seating host or hostess. Since my husband was raised with traditional good manners, he is always the last to the table. Even though he is the one with the personal need to have a specific seat, being the last to the table always creates the havoc with everyone moving around so that Dad can have his certain seat. Square tables are okay, round tables are more difficult, usually ending up where all five of us are shifting by one or two chairs. People arriving for dinner being seated at the same time as us are probably well into their meals by the time the seating at our table is acceptable.

If it's just the two of us, I try to think ahead so it's a quicker process but I tend to forget sometimes and then he just stands there and looks at me instead of sitting first. Sigh, sometimes marriage really sucks.

One thing I cannot concede. If we are at a hotel, depending on how the bathroom is situated, left or right of the bed, he must give in to my demands. I don't care what anyone says, husbands and wives have certain sides of the bed to sleep on no matter where they are. My husband has always had the right side of the bed, I have the left. But this may change in a hotel. I will always require the side nearest the bathroom. I don't know why, perhaps a habit I acquired from my pregnancy days. I really believe that's when I became claustrophobic. Or possibly some other kind of phobia, I don't know. But my husband, being a smart man, gives in to me on that and never complains. I think he knows that's one he can't win. But actually he's just a pretty nice guy when he wants to be. Well really, he just knows when to fight his battles and when to just give in to me. We've been together for 26 years after all.

Leading to the point that one of the reasons why my marriage has worked all these years is because I believe I give him 51% and I let him have better, more, etcetera. My husband also believes he gives me 51% as well. With that kind of consideration we can't lose. Unless we're fighting; on that day, there may or may not be consideration.

When we're at a movie theater, he always lets me pick the row and a seat first. However, I move over so much that he still can get the middle seat in front of the screen. It's nice because our children have learned this and will do the same for each other. On that same note, my husband will always hold the door open for anybody waiting to go inside an establishment. Our children have learned this and will do the same. It is very nice to see young people being considerate in this modern age of everyone in a hurry and everyone for themselves. But they've also learned to be critical of rude people from their dad, the cop. Most of the time our children will just get disgusted and say "People!"

Now that I've introduced the topic of our children, that's where things changed in our ratio. When children came along, I had to find a happy medium to our ratio. No matter what, mom comes last. The husband eats, the children eat, and mom eats last. My husband always liked to wait and eat with me so in our household, the children ate first. It was hard for me since I grew up in a traditional household where my Dad was served first. But this was the way my husband wanted it so it's how we do it. The nights where we actually get to sit as a family at the table together for a meal are very few now. With our children's schedules and my husband's and my own all being so different, it's a rare treat to sit together. At Olive Garden, the seating host or hostess will always ask if there is a special occasion that we are celebrating when the five of us happen to go to eat there. I say yes, the special occasion is that we are all together for a meal!

Back to 51:49. As we grow older, we are so accustomed to each other and our habits, our likes and dislikes, our unusual behaviors and moods depending on the day, that we can behave very selfish at times. The difference is that we are now more forgiving of these times and will not dwell on them so much as when we were young. Our feelings were hurt so much easier back then, because our love was so brand new and we were actually so brand new to each other. When we were newlyweds and had a fight, it was the end of the world, or the end of our marriage. It hurt so much that we felt we must have been disillusioned to have married each other. Now I understand "disillusionment of marriage" or dissolution of marriage—what the common reason used in a divorce is called and why it is used. I truly believe some people should not be married and that no matter how hard one partner may try to keep a marriage together, if the other partner is not agreeable, it could not possibly work.

We still believe in 51:49 but we don't dwell on it, it's just a way of life for us. Like respect. But once in a while, when I'm feeling very selfish or crabby, I need to remind myself of my mother's advice. She still lives with this philosophy and though she speaks her mind to my father now more than when she was younger, she still puts my father first. My father does the same with my mother even though I never really thought of it so much when I was younger. It's because he's always so busy hustling here and there and working that it always seemed like he never considered my mother. And maybe it is something that my father has learned over the years as they've grown older together. But it is very sweet when I see my father taking care of my mother and being considerate of her needs.

So in another chapter I've mentioned that my husband has told me in the past that it seems to him that I keep score on things we do for each other. I've never consciously decided to do that, however, I see his point. Even by writing this chapter about 51:49, I must be keeping some kind of track of things I do for him. So I do not have a score, like a tally sheet or something foolish like that. But in my mind, I do make sure I mentally stop myself when I think he's being selfish. Sometimes it works and other times it doesn't. I don't think my husband is a selfish person at all. I do think that he dwells on a lot of negative factors and that negativity creates some bad feelings between us. He has become a man who looks at a glass as being half empty instead of half full. He wasn't this man when we first became married but I believe the daily grind of his job has created this negativity in him.

So I do my best at home to make him see things differently. Sometimes I try too hard and we end up in a yelling match—Wrong! Not really the best way to convince someone they're being negative, by screaming it at him. His bullheaded and unreasonable stance can really bring out the screaming banshee in me sometimes. I know, sometimes marriage really sucks for him too.

It's not always easy to maintain this ratio and even though it becomes second nature after a while, especially if the love is still there, it's still hard to live it every day. I'm not perfect and there are days that I just don't care if he comes first or not. This can be true of any day, whether we are fighting or not fighting. But lucky for me, my husband loves me too and he will pick up the reigns and put me first. It's on those days that I truly appreciate him. He doesn't understand my mood swings, what man can really understand a woman's mood swings? Women don't even understand them! But my husband does his best to try and sometimes he succeeds. He does not succeed every time but he isn't perfect either. The best we can hope for is to continue the struggle to stay true and good to each other. And live to fight another day? I wish I could say we wouldn't but I'm a believer in not kidding myself.

Ken & Essay. September 1986.

Douglas James: 6 months; 5 years; 17 years; 25 years.

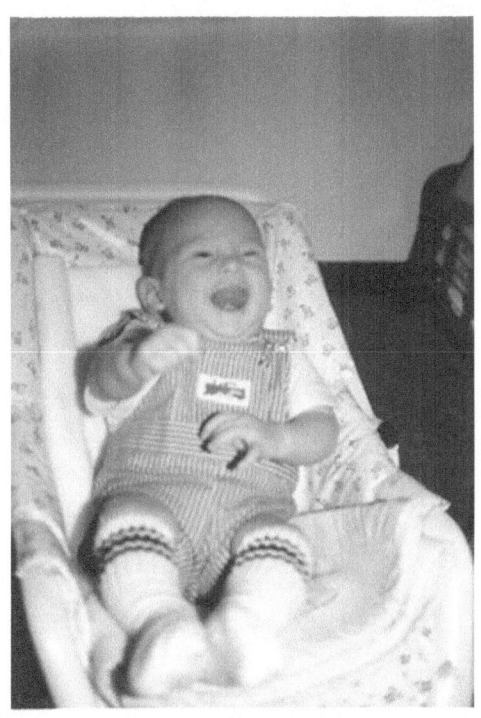

Pamela Jo: 8 months; 3 years; 17 years; 22 years.

Sarah Jean: 9 months; 7 years; 17 years; 17 years.

Doug, Pam, Sarah at Halloween and Christmas.

Family at Easter; Family at Wyoming.

Ken & Essay.

Essay & sisters. Left to right, top to bottom: Essay, Becky, Sharon, Shirley.

Essay's parents, LaVerne and Fusako, 1965.

Springer/Retriever "Fancy." Cats "Caesar and Cleopatra."

Chapter Six

The In-laws

I have three sisters. We all have in-laws. I never dreamed that I would be the only one with the proverbial in-law problems. Sometimes in-laws really suck.

I am the oldest of four girls to a Dad and Mom who were farmers. No sons. So I was the son. I cultivated fields and learned to operate and drive a tractor and certain farm implements from the age of 8. I had little patience with my younger siblings while growing up since none of them were required to do the same. Shirley, my sister closest in age to me, had rheumatic fever at the age of 7 and almost died, so was never very robust as a child. She was not required to do heavy farm work. Sharon was 5 years younger and by the time she was old enough, we had moved off the farm into town. Becky was, and still is the baby being eight years my junior.

I didn't mind being the one to do the work outdoors but I also had to look out for and babysit the girls. Sometimes I was short with them, I remember always being angry and stern with them (I don't know how they can stand me!), and I remember Shirley always trying (and succeeding) to get me in trouble.

Even though I enjoyed spending time with my Dad, busy as he always was, I longed to be in the house and play with my dolls, play dress-up, do crafts and artwork, all the girly things to do. So I loved the rainy days—Shirley and I would take out our Barbies and every other doll and teddy bear we owned and make up stories and create a lovely (or sometimes scary) world for our dolls. It would be a fairy tale world but having, apparently, watched too much TV, our married dolls all had in-law problems. The mother-in-law never liked the girl or the boy, whichever was the case. But this was make-believe and we never really believed in it. Like evil stepmothers and scary witches and wish granting fairy god-mothers, it wasn't real.

The Andrew Family (my family) get-togethers, for holidays or re-unions or whatever occasion we chose to celebrate, were very mild parties. We drank Kool-Aid or coffee, we ate cake and pie or watermelon. If we stopped by Grandma and Grandpa's unexpectedly and Grandma had no cake, then she would have soda crackers with frosting between them or Cheez Whiz or just plain oleo margarine. It was all delicious; we were very happy grandchildren and loved to get together with the family.

Sometimes our cousins and uncles and aunts would be visiting from anywhere in Kansas, South Dakota, and Missouri or just down the road. If it was summer, the grownups would sit under the oak trees in lawn chairs and drink coffee or iced tea and smoke cigarettes. The kids would be running around the lawn and the barns looking for kittens or chasing the mean rooster or playing hide and seek. Later after dark, the grown-ups would play whist or hearts at the kitchen table and the kids would color in coloring books or play with dolls or with the set of metal farm implements and barn animals. There was no alcohol (maybe a can of beer or two in the hot summer days outside with watermelon and potato salad) but no one missed it. There were no problems, none that I can remember. No crying, no leaving in a huff, no heated arguments (unless it was an election year, just kidding), really, I feel now that I've led a sheltered life.

My husband first met my extended family (grandparents, cousins, aunts and uncles) at my Grandparent's 50th wedding anniversary. We both dressed up (I wore a yellow dress and heels and Ken wore a brown sports jacket and dress pants) and I didn't realize this would make my family think that Ken was a snob. Anyway, that passed over quickly and he fit in with my family very well. My Grandfather teased Ken about being a Swede (my Grandfather being mostly German and English) but he told Ken that he was okay. He called Ken a "white" Swede. Take that as you will. Grandpa was a bit of a red-neck. Grandpa always sat at the kitchen table in his usual chair with a 22 rifle so he could shoot the squirrels in the bird feeders from the kitchen window. Grandma always just sighed. She sighed a lot. Now that I've been married so long, I find myself sighing a lot. I guess it's just something we've learned to do when we can't change them. "Them" being the men in our lives. Can't change 'em, can't shoot 'em . . . is that how the phrase goes?

Ken and I had only been dating about a month when I first met his parents. Ken's parents came to our college for a visit and to meet me. It was Ken's birthday in February and they came to take us both out to dinner. It was a very nice dinner and I felt good about it. Ken's father was a man of few words, not unlike a lot of men of his generation. His father was the same age as my Grandma, and he served in World War II, so he was much older than my Dad, who served in Vietnam. Ken's mother also was very quiet but I could tell she was crazy about Ken and wanted as much information as she could gather about anything and everything that was Ken. Ken is the baby of his family. This I could understand and I didn't mind. At that first meeting, I found that I liked them a lot.

Two months later, in April, Ken and I went to his sister's house in the twin cities area and there I was to meet the rest of his immediate family. Ken has one sister and two brothers. It was Easter and the dinner was at his sister's house. She and her three young girls were busy preparing food, Ken's mother and I helped, his older brother and his girlfriend tried staying out of the way, and his oldest brother and his wife and two kids were late. Apparently they are always late, I was told. They showed up and I could see she had been crying and he looked angry. Not a great start. I didn't ask any questions.

Half way through the meal, Ken got up and walked out. He just disappeared. I was with the kids and didn't even know he was gone until his mother and sister and sister-in-law found me and demanded to know where he went. I was confused and said I didn't know. Then the crying and the yelling started. His mother was crying and saying that it was all her own fault, she must have said something wrong. His sister and sister-in-law were pretending not to look at each other; I could see that they didn't get along. Needless to say, I was pissed! How dare he just walk out and leave me to this! And we weren't even married yet, that guy had some explaining to do!

I went out and started walking down the street. After a couple blocks, I found him walking a side street. I asked him what was going on. He wouldn't answer me. I told him that I was the stranger here, I was the guest. This is not how I need to be treated. WHAT IS GOING ON HERE? He said "couldn't you hear it?" Hear what? He said the fight was just going to get started. That the women were just starting to pick on each other and the undertones were more than he could handle. I said GREAT! And you would leave me to that? How was that okay? He apologized and I made him swear that if it ever happened again, he had better take me with him. I also told him that if the fight hadn't started before he walked out, it certainly has started since. Good job, babe.

Though I'm not a tea-totaler, because I love an occasional glass of wine or even a mixed drink, I do believe that alcohol is the root of a lot of evil, a lot of miss-haps. To this day, if I drink an extra glass of wine too much, I will say goofy and inappropriate things. Things I regret later. That is because alcohol is the great uninhibitor. Ken's brother that is two years his senior is simply a mean and unhappy drunk and should never drink a drop of alcohol, not even beer. He reverts back to his childhood when kids on the bus would pick on him and he felt inferior to his little brother Ken because Ken was more popular. Ken's oldest brother gets frisky and I'm always running away from his amorous advances. Or he gets lost in corn fields. That's a long story. Ken's sister and sister-in-law apparently get into fights, saying things to each other that they may or may not regret later, I don't remember why they hate each other.

One Christmas I experienced a terrible exchange between Ken and his brother because of alcohol and his brother wanted to give his baby brother a snow-wash. Older brother ended up actually on the receiving end when Ken got through with him. Then older brother screamed obscenities at everyone and left with his new wife and two week old infant. Ken's mother ran upstairs in a crying fit, and Ken's father yelled at Ken for causing a scene. Ken and I, who were living with his parents at the time having just come back from some active duty Army training, quietly packed up our belongings and found an apartment and moved out the very week after New Year's. I was shocked and terribly confused at the horrible Christmas Eve scene but I totally understood and supported Ken when he said he wanted nothing to do with his brother after that. Even though his mother tried bullying them for years to speak to each other, the brothers stay separate to this day. They see each other on occasion for weddings, reunions, graduations and funerals, and then say very little to each other. It's sad, but necessary.

Ken's father died in 1995 of dementia and complications from a very bad heart surgery that resulted in several strokes. His mother died in 2011 of complications due to emphysema and several other health issues. Ken did not speak to his mother for 2 years before she died. Even on her death bed, he did not visit her. Did I ever say that my husband holds a grudge and is very stubborn? His mother lived with his sister for the last 16 years of her life, ever since his father died. It was a mutual living situation. His sister worked and his mother cooked and took care of the house. I thought it was a good situation with the two of them fighting often but I knew they couldn't live without each other. Two years previous to her death, Ken's mother approached us about wanting to move out and live in assisted Senior Housing. We said we would be glad to help, apparently his mother and sister were again fighting and his mother couldn't live with her anymore. Anytime we had dinner or got together with his mother, she always complained about her daughter. We took it in stride—his mother forever loved to be a martyr and always felt she was overworked and unappreciated.

When Ken's mother asked us about senior housing, we told her what we knew would happen. With only Social Security to live on (she did not get to keep her husband's retirement pension after his death), the state would have to pay for her living. This meant that she would have a very limited bank account and maybe not even be able to keep her vehicle. We told her this, because my Grandmother had just done the same that very year. What his mother took home from this, was to tell his sister, and all her other children, that Ken and I wanted to keep her car. Of course his sister in-law called Ken immediately and told him this, loving to be the bearer of bad news and hear people's reactions first hand. His own sister confirmed it, yes, the one that his mother needed to get away from. When Ken confronted his mother, she vehemently denied it and said they were all lying and she didn't know why everyone was against her. Ken told her he was done with her and that he was tired of her lying and manipulating him. I was very sad for my husband but I supported him. I did not go see his mother behind his back. But two weeks before she died, I'm very glad that I did go see her. She was so happy to see me that she cried. Of course she asked for Ken and went on and on about why he didn't believe her. I said that he was his father's son and who could explain men? She seemed okay with that answer. I did not want to spend my last visit with her arguing about her lack of character and poor decisions made in the past. She would not have understood and it would not have been the right thing to do at the time. I truly believe she did not know that she did anything wrong.

The funeral was a terrible fiasco and it wouldn't have been able to happen if I didn't take out my credit card at the funeral home and offer to pay for it because of course his oldest brother and wife were very late. His second brother paid $50 because that's all he could afford and his sister-in-law, wife of oldest brother said they booked the VFW for afterwards so that amount should come out so I guess that means the funeral home doesn't get paid the rest? So who's supposed to absorb the rest of the cost of the funeral? Foolish, foolish people. No worries, the youngest brother's wife can cover the cost of her mother-in-law's funeral. I did it for his mother's sake—not for them. I did love her after all these years because I really believe she never realized how her actions affected her son. She really loved him and never knew how much she hurt him over the years.

My family is very different than Ken's. My family is not perfect but we do everything out of a deep love and concern for each other. If we tell each other some bad news, it will not get spread around. We show care and concern and try to find ways to help each other. Maybe it's because we are a younger family. When Ken and I first got married, my sister's ages were 19, 16, and 12; my parents were in their 40's, just a couple years older than Ken's oldest brother and wife. Ken was the hero of my little sisters, the brother they never had. They look up to him to this day—especially my baby sister Becky who was only 12 when she first met him. All she did was giggle and laugh when he was around. My dad was more a big brother to Ken than a father and my mother is his very favorite—my husband will do anything for my mom. When we were first married, Ken could never walk in the door of their house without my Mom asking him if he was hungry within the first 5 minutes. She doted on him, cooked his favorite meals, made sure he was comfortable and taken care of.

My mother is a petite Japanese lady, very traditional, believing that the father is the head of the household and all things revolve around him. He is served meals first, he is served ice cream first, he gets control of the TV, he decides when and where to go to shop for groceries or school clothes or even where to go to church. I remember when I was 11 years old my mother was baptized along with my father, full emersion baptism, in a Baptist Church. My mother was a Buddhist, as was her entire family in Japan. She told me that she will believe in whatever God my father believes in. That's how important my father is to her and how important his decisions are to her. My father is a good man and has never taken advantage of my mother's belief in him. He always discussed his decisions with her, even knowing that she will support whatever he decides. It's just the right thing to do and they both respect each other a great deal.

Because my mother is a gentle person, and a good person, she always listens very well. She may or may not give me advice, usually giving advice only when asked. My father is the same. They both believe in "minding their own business" and have taught all of us girls the same. They are not pushy people, they do not judge anybody. This doesn't mean they love all people, they are not saints! But they respected Ken's decision to separate himself from his family and asked no questions.

My parents and sisters care very much about the family as I do myself. None of us likes to gossip or spread bad news about each other. When one sister is having marital problems, we all support her and we do not say bad things about her husband. It's sad because no matter what we think about that one sister's husband, we all know how much she still loves him, and if we bash him we will only be hurting her. This we will never do so we all refrain from saying anything negative about my sister's estranged husband, for her sake.

I remember when my youngest sister had a boyfriend, I'll call him Steve. He was more than just a boyfriend; he became the father of her only child. They wanted to marry but unfortunately he was an alcoholic and my sister told him he must sober up and stay sober and keep a job before she would consider it. It's actually very sad because they really loved each other. But he could not stay sober and keep a job. When he tried to be sober, he was depressed and then they would fight. They were not good together both times they tried living together. But it was sad too because the family loved him. He was funny and loved to play with all the kids. My three children thought he was the best and always looked forward to seeing him. My husband enjoyed talking with him and I know both my parents liked him as well. I had a lot of fun conversations with him and we got to be good friends, I thought.

When Steve and my sister broke up for good, he called me on the phone to talk about it. Actually he wanted to talk about her. I listened for a while and then I asked him what it was that he wanted me to say? I told him that even though I know my sister's shortcomings, I could never say anything bad about her. I told him that if he was asking me to choose between the two of them, I would always be on her side, even if she is in the wrong. It is because we are sisters, a bond that cannot be broken or betrayed. I knew this hurt him very much and I was very sad about it, liking him very much too, but I could never hurt my sister by having a discussion about her behind her back with her ex-lover. He never called me again. Maybe it was better that way. It hurts my sister very much, to this day, because she has not been able to get over him. I know it is who she compares all her dates with, and she cannot find anyone who is as funny or charismatic to be with. It's just too bad he can't stay away from his drinking. He is actually a pretty good carpenter when sober.

I hope my sisters forgive me for using them as examples but the reason why I included the two stories about two sisters is to explain how my family supports and cares about each other. It is very important and a lesson that we have all learned from our parents. Something I hope my husband and I can teach our children now that they are older and have already a great difference of feelings towards each other. There are no in-laws yet, none of my children are as yet married. It frightens me about when that day will come, how we will all behave with each other, especially with grandchildren to share. I only hope that Ken and I will behave as my parents do, doing all things with love and care and concern.

So in conclusion of this chapter about the in-laws, I just believe that I married a good man. No matter what I may think of his family—his parents, brothers, or sister—I always remember the man I married and will try to behave as my mother would. I will try to keep supporting him and his decisions. I might try nudging him a little this way or that, but not too much. I have not included any names of my in-laws because I am not trying to hurt any of them, only trying to make a point with my stories. I found that in my life people don't necessarily like the truth, so they create a truth they can live with. Or not, I'm no expert.

Chapter Seven

Having Money Problems?

My husband and I started our lives together with no plan and no money. We were young and terribly in love and thought everything would just work out. Or maybe it was only me thinking that way and he just went along—he really did seem very dazed and confused that first year of marriage. Confused like he didn't know where he was or why he was there. I wonder if that's a normal guy thing or just my husband. I realize I can be very bossy and just automatically believe that everyone thinks like I do.

My husband never really asked me to marry him. We started as acquaintances that had every College Army ROTC class together and with both of us being high achievers, we also signed up for all the extra-curriculars. We soon became best friends and were totally there for each other, having a deep respect and trust for each other. Our senior year, we accidentally went on a date, just the two of us, no other group of friends with us, and decided we liked it! So we went out on more dates. Then we decided to look at engagement rings. Then he came to dinner at my parent's house and asked my mom and dad for my hand in marriage—we are very old fashioned. This was new to my parents as I was their oldest daughter. My dad said "You're a nice guy, I like you, okay." (These were his exact words; I remember them to this day!) My mom just nodded and sniffed her tears back. My three younger sisters were huddled downstairs trying to hear every word above their giggles.

Somehow, we both knew we were getting married without having to say it out loud. There was no one else in the world for us. This was it, we each knew we were through looking and had found our perfect match. Still, to this day I wonder if he was just waiting for me to ask him to marry him. And I was waiting for him to ask me. So no one asked. Strange, I know.

So we got married, six months after our engagement which was one month after our first date. We had no money. We were very lucky to be able to afford a two bedroom apartment that we only qualified for since we were still part-time college students and received a discounted rate. It was $250.00 a month, which I remember back in 1986 was a huge amount to us. Especially when I wasn't working, Ken had only a part-time job paying minimum wage (barely $4.00/hour) at a jewelry store and we were expecting a baby on the way! Thinking back, I realize now it was a foolish way to start out, but we did it. My parents helped us out with some groceries when they could but at that time they still had my three sisters (19, 16, and 12) at home and were struggling as well.

Ken got into a Guard Unit first and then I did after Digger was born and then the money problems cleared up a little. We spent 6 months together in Army Officer Basic Course training (a requirement for all newly commissioned 2nd Lieutenants) in Huntsville, Alabama, and that was very difficult for me. We had to leave Digger with Ken's parents for that time and he was only 15 months old when we left him. I had a picture of him in my work area every day and Ken hated taking me to the Laundromat or the Mall or anywhere there may be babies or toddlers because I would start getting all moon eyed and my hands would start itching like I would steal one of them. Only if they had light tan skin color and light brown curly hair and a perfectly cute baby face! Actually they all looked that way to me, I was going a little crazy.

Six months later, we were able to go home in December, our training complete. We had to give up the lease to our apartment and had all our possessions in storage at his parent's home so we lived with them for a while.

The first thing I noticed was that Digger really didn't remember Mommy and Daddy very well. He was calling his grandparents Momma and Papa and though Daddy was not a similar word, Momma and Mommy were very confusing for a 22 month old baby. I insisted he call me momma and his grandmother was now grandma (she was not happy). The clincher was when we were shopping and poor baby Digger was so confused about who was Mommy that he started calling all random women Mommy. The checkout lady was mommy, the old lady we walked past who was shopping was mommy; he was a very friendly baby and said hi to everyone.

After a family fall-out at the fateful Christmas that year, we moved out into an apartment near the city within two weeks after Christmas. It was a rushed move, but we were so happy once we had our own apartment again. We had saved as much money as we could from our very good temporary duty pay as Army officers and was living on that until Ken got a job working security. He was very shortly admitted into the city's police academy that same summer and he has been working as a cop for the city ever since. It's been 23 years now that he has been with the city. He is a good cop. The pay has been capped for years now but he has pretty decent benefits and a good retirement.

Funny thing about money is that our situation is always so fluid. One year we are coasting, no money problems and we have some breathing space. We can buy the big screen TV and new tires for both vehicles and not go into big debt on our credit cards. The next year we are struggling a little and must pinch back. It's probably me. I'm so terrible with a budget. Over the years I have made out budget plans, several of them, but do I have to stick to them? That is my problem. I'm not good with a long term plan. We have money today, I must spend it tomorrow. I still make sure all bills are paid on time. But we have nothing left over. Thank goodness for our retirement pensions.

I started working full time for a major retailer 15 years ago. 9 years ago I decided to become salaried, receiving a promotion and then working very long hours. I had little time for my children or husband and 13 of the last 15 years have been on third shift so I didn't even get to sleep with my husband for most of those years! I was promoted yet again three years ago and my work hours increased to 60 hours per week, sometimes more. But my salary also increased—I had never earned so much money and my income became the major contributor to our household. However, though our financial situation became much less inhibited, we spent little time together and also spent more time eating out, spending more money yet again.

So what's the happy medium? Is it better to be happy and poor or to be unhappy, tired, crabby, and comfortably well-off? I believe this is a problem for most households where mom and dad both work. It would be so very nice to have it all—to have money and to have time. Is that even 1% of the population of the US? I don't really know the demographics of that but I do know that it is very rare to have both time and money.

So we make do. We find time for one family vacation per year. We make time to go to school events and weddings and the zoo. And we enjoy this time so much because it is so rare and so dear to us. We become sad because our children grow up so fast and wasn't it just yesterday that they were Digger and Jo-Jo and Peanut? We wonder where those years went and wish we had that time back even though during the time of the formula and diapers and being up all night we were wishing the babies would grow up quicker.

Many of the fights between my husband and me are about money. I really don't understand why that is true. Our money situation is what it is. It is very true that my husband is frugal and I am not. It is similar to our true nature, our personalities. My husband is quiet and conservative in nature. I am emotional and impulsive. We have a great respect for each other, my husband always wanting to be more outgoing, a little like me. I always want to be able to sit and think things through better, weigh all the angles like my husband.

A perfect example is with board games. I always make my husband read the instructions and then explain it to all of us after he's done reading them because he's so thorough and can completely understand it. I will read some of the instructions and just start playing because I am impatient and just want to get going. Then we make mistakes along the way and I don't care, it's just a game. This drives my husband crazy! So we just do it his way and it works out for all of us. I don't have to try to understand the long-winded instructions and Ken gets to be his thorough self.

However, this does not work with the instructions on the assembly of furniture. He will look at the instructions so far as to how many pieces of each item he should have to start with. He usually ends up with extra pieces or something doesn't fit properly and there is a lot of swearing. We have been married for 26 years and he still won't look at the factory instructions when assembling. This frustrates me to no end and I've finally decided that I will be assembling the furniture going forward. I've recently purchased a new futon couch. I remembered how much swearing happened when Ken assembled our last one. So I opened the instructions and assembled it with some help from Peanut. I didn't have any pieces left over and I didn't have to swear. The best part is that I didn't have to endure Ken's swearing! Yay! It only took 26 years for me to figure this out—wow, am I a slow learner.

My husband does place a lot of trust in me with our finances; however, no matter how much I may joke about our differences. He does not like to gamble. I do like to gamble. Penny slots are my favorite. This began during our 19th year of marriage. I was going through some kind of depression with long hours at work and rude teenagers and a messy house and an unusually large amount of fighting with Ken. I went to the nearest casino, a Native American Reservation run casino, with a friend of mine. I enjoyed just playing penny slots, maybe 20 cents at a time. I spent anywhere around $20 to $40, win or lose. Some mornings after work, I would drive the 45 minutes there to wind down before going home. It was mindless. I could forget work, kids, husband, and just push a button. I told my husband once that it was cheaper therapy than a psychiatrist. So he listened, and allowed it without fuss. Of course he likes when I win and is unhappy when I lose, and he knows I spend much more than just $20 or $40 now, but he still trusts me to know how much I can spend and still take care of our finances. That's actually a lot of trust and I know I can't fail him. It's what keeps me from over-spending at the casino, which is very easy to do.

I believe our arguing over finances has calmed down considerably with age, and of course, with better finances. The only times when my husband gets upset now is during those family vacations when he knows I've saved cash and have a certain amount on our credit cards allowed for our expenses but he will still say, throughout the entire vacation that we should never have come. It costs too much. It's not worth the cost. On and on and on. It certainly dampens the fun. Then when vacation is over and what we have are the memories and pictures to look at and reminisce about, he says that it was fun and he's glad we went. Wow, sometimes marriage really sucks . . .

We go through cycles of having money and having no money, but we manage to survive. It's not something that will break up our marriage. We have so much of everything else. If you don't consider an actual dollar amount, we are very rich in our marriage. So come on, let's say it. Sometimes money, having it or not having it, really sucks!

Chapter Eight

Oh no! He's got a Cold!

Why is it that when a husband is sick, the world is ending? You would think that a big strong man can handle anything that comes his way. He can handle everything except for a little small bacterium that creates havoc with his manly world. This little bacterium makes him go back to his childhood—this is when the wife must be "mommy". And no matter how many years you've been married, this will never change. So if you are a newlywed, get ready for it and get used to it!

Actually, the first time I experienced my husband being sick was before we were married. We were dating at the time and he called me and said he couldn't come over to see me because he had a cold and a fever. He sounded miserable. I went over to the house he shared with three other guys, cleaned the messy kitchen so that I had clean pots, counters, and stove to cook on, made him some homemade chicken dumpling soup and fed him. He lay on the couch with a pillow and blanket and the remote control while I fed him hot soup. Now that I think back on that memory, that occasion might have been the clincher as to why he decided to marry me. Quite possibly. Most likely.

I may make a point of mentioning how men become babies when they're sick, but women kind of bring this behavior on themselves. I mean, really, I didn't have to rush right over and cook him hot soup. I could have just left him alone like he asked. But I am positive that he did not want to be left alone with his cold and fever. He had a tone in his voice that called out to a certain instinct that I possessed that took over my actions and made me run to his house and take care of him. So I realize it is my own fault that all those many years ago I contributed to a behavior that he maintains to this day. He knows that if he says he is sick, I will drop everything and take over. I will find out all his aches and pains, and I will react accordingly. The only part that he stays stubborn about is that when I suggest that he sees a doctor for something that sounds serious, he will refuse to go. Is this all men? I know my father will refuse to go to a doctor and if he does go, then it is very serious indeed. The same is with my husband.

So I'm beginning to wonder if he just needs to complain about certain aches and pains because he will gain sympathy from me and the symptoms may not be quite as serious as he makes them out to be. Is this a man trick? It's probably just plain human nature. I'm sure there are men out there that never complain about a cold. I've never met one but I'm sure they must be out there. There are anomalies for every situation, so there must be one somewhere.

I guess it's a good thing that men are the way they are. God must have had this preordained for womankind. To prepare us for raising children, of course! It may be a bigger package but inside it's all the same goo.

The toughest is when we are fighting and he is being stubborn and won't end the fight, or vice-versa. He will use the excuse that he doesn't feel good. Then he knows I will give in and take care of him because I really do care. I might resist for a whole 5 minutes but it's really agonizing for me to not respond to his pain. Now keep in mind that by the phrase "his pain", I'm meaning the "not feeling so good" pain. If he has pain because I threw a hairbrush at him or something, then that is good and I won't tend to that. No, that's not true either. When we make up after the fight, then I will tend to any wounds that may have occurred during the fight. Actually, I don't remember if this has actually happened but I know I would do that. I'm always sorry after a fight that has started over something stupid. Not the fights that count though. Every marriage has personal things that happen where no matter how long the time has passed the memory of the hurt remains. We have some of those too. Sometimes it's hard to forgive AND forget. Sometimes we just forgive. Alzheimer's will help us forget later, I guess.

How do I react when I'm sick? I just crawl in bed and I want to be left alone. Don't expect me to cook or clean or solve problems or to even talk. Just let me curl up and die! I don't want anyone to take care of me and to ask me what I need or to feel sorry for me. This also applies to my migraines that I succumb to every once in a while. No sound, no light, no movement by me or around me—really, or I will vomit! Just leave me alone until I feel human again. Why are men and women so very different? Or it could just be me, I suppose.

Let us now discuss aches and pains. We all suffer from body aches and pains as we grow older. It seems that my husband actually hoards his aches and pains—kind of like he wants to keep them to constantly remind me that he is older than me. My husband is almost exactly 4 ½ years older than me. The reason why I say that he keeps them is that he won't do anything about curing them. His doctors and I have been after him for the last 15 years to get knee surgery done. He has no ACL in one knee; his meniscus is busted up and keeps catching in his knee joint on his other knee so he is constantly in pain or getting his leg locked up.

My husband works part-time off-duty police jobs. If he has knee surgery, this would put him on a desk job and off the streets for at least 6 months. It would also mean that he could not work any off-duty jobs. So this was his excuse for many years to not be able to have the knee surgery done. But in the last three years, he has worked very little part-time jobs, largely due to the fact that my position was given a raise and he didn't have the need for them. But he still refuses to have knee surgery.

This leads me to believe that he may actually have a possible fear of surgery. It's understandable, I would fear it. There are several things to fear: the fear that the surgery may not correct his knees and they may become even worse, the fear of anesthetics or just the plain fear of going under the knife. But he won't admit that. So I'm just left with the complaining and the fact that he can't run, play sports, or even go on hikes and walks with me. He just always says that he's old, like he's been saying since the age of 26 just because he's older than me.

I try to help him stay healthier by giving him a vigorous daily vitamin regimen. He takes daily multivitamins, fish oil, glucosamine for joints, prostate pills, fiber, and anything else I can find that sounds good and healthy. And I have purchased several different kinds of ACE bandages and knee supports to help him to also include joint creams. If these don't help him nothing will. Nothing will short of knee surgery.

He also suffers from sciatica from years of wearing his leather police belt with 30 pounds of weight around his waist. This flares up when he stands for long periods of time, especially during the holidays when he is directing a lot of traffic in and out of parking lots. This requires a lot of high dosages of ibuprofen to help with the pain. I actually succeeded in getting him a doctor's appointment for this. Unfortunately, this doctor did not listen to any of my husband's actual symptoms and just sent him on an MRI which cost us almost $1000.00 out of pocket expense to tell us nothing. Of course, this arrogant doctor has successfully ended any other attempts for me to get my husband to see anyone else. So I endure more daily moaning and groaning from my husband.

I may joke about my husband's pain but it is really no laughing matter. I do not like to see him in pain, from symptoms that I cannot help him get better. I can help him combat the common cold virus, strep throat, or even the flu. Allergies, rashes, ear and sinus infections, even walking pneumonia; these I can help him fight. I can even crack his back and help him re-align. But the knees, sciatica, those that require much more than "doctor mom" can handle, about these he remains stubborn. I'm still working on getting those knees done. It's a weekly argument and I will eventually wear him down. It's been 15 years already. It might take 20 but he will eventually succumb to my persistence. He may be stubborn, but I am the master manipulator. I think all wives are and now I'm giving away my mother's secret. Hope I don't get in trouble . . .

Chapter Nine

Family holidays, vacations, and the zoo . . .

As a child, my family went to many get-togethers with neighbors and friends and relatives. It was always fun, my parents are very out-going and neighborly—no matter where we lived, they made friends quickly and everyone loved them. So we had no shortage of invitations to visit people every week.

But when it came to vacations, it seemed that the years that Dad had the extra money, we didn't have the time or there were the years with no extra money. And with 6 of us, vacations were costly. So we didn't do vacations or trips with the exception of the spring of my senior year in high school. We went on a road trip vacation to the Ozarks in Missouri to visit my Dad's sister and her family. My Aunt and Uncle and four cousins lived outside Fort Leonard-Wood Missouri in a small town called Newburg, my uncle having retired from the Army and that was his last post. It was a great vacation, lasting about a week, with some lovely memories.

Because I loved that one family vacation so much, I wanted to make sure our kids had the opportunity to have those same lovely memories. Our first family vacation was to the Black Hills in South Dakota and our children were 10, 6, and 16 months. We were only there for four days but it was a great time, the hotel had a swimming pool shaped like Mickey Mouse's head and the kids spent a lot of time in it. They enjoyed Bear Country where we drove through the preserve and laughed at the funny things that real bears do. They enjoyed Mount Rushmore though we didn't climb it, the funniest being just the drive there with the wild mountain goats and buffalos along the side of the road. Parents must enjoy their time with their children while they are young and everything is funny or silly. It gets more difficult to entertain them when they grow into teenagers.

We went back to the Black Hills again, as a family, years later when the kids were 16, 12, and 7. Not quite as easy to entertain them, but we still had a good time. This time we made fun of silly things like a man dressed up like Abraham Lincoln at Mount Rushmore who pinched my butt when we took a picture with him. We laughed hysterically when we stopped to shop at the local Wal-Mart and were behind a man who didn't realize his running shorts were bunched up so that one cheek was exposed. Actually, yikes, but we laughed anyway. When the kids are small you make them turn away from such things or don't tell them about it. When they are teens you point and laugh or like us, just hold it and laugh afterwards. Or just try not to be too obvious. This was also the trip when we were in the darkest part of Jewel Caves and the lights were turned off so we had complete darkness and complete sound depravation. We were supposed to be listening to the living sounds of the cave. All we heard at the time was the sound of a fart from the direction of three elderly ladies standing on one corner of the platform to our left. The poor tour guide was trying hard to have everyone be quiet and "listen to the sounds of the cave". The little kids that were part of the tour could not stop snickering and laughing so he finally gave up trying. Oh well, it's a memory.

In between those years of the Black Hills, we went to Atlanta, Georgia, to visit my sister. The kids were 14, 10 and 5. It was in the spring, on spring break from school, so we spent the Easter holiday with my sister and her husband and his family. My sister has great in-laws that have taken good care of her over the years, she being so very far away from the rest of her family. Her in-laws have adopted all of us and we always enjoy visiting them in Georgia. We visited the Atlanta Zoo and Stone Mountain. We visited Antebellum Plantations with old slave quarters. The kids were still young enough that they just went along with whatever mom and dad said and we had a good time. Plus we rode on the airplane there and back which was an adventure for the family as well. This is something we should have remembered in future, this "riding the airplane" versus "road-trip".

We went to Georgia two more times over the years, when the kids were older, the last trip being about three years ago. We drove both times. It was actually not bad, except for the time we had to go through Louisville, Kentucky, and stay at a Quality Inn when the Final Four was in town. All hotels were solidly booked, we had a suite since we booked several months ahead of time and there are five of us. But our room was shabby and dirty and when we pulled out the hide-a-bed couch and found dirty sheets on it, we went to the front desk and complained. All they said was "here's some sheets, make the bed yourself". Yuck! So we've never stayed at an Un-Quality Inn since then. We left, got a refund after my husband yelled at the manager (my husband's very scary when he's angry), and we slept in our vehicle at a wayside rest area. On this second trip we drove down to Savannah to see the ocean. We enjoyed that so much that the third trip down we booked a hotel in advance and spent the night. We went on a haunted bus tour of the city, stopping at cemeteries and outside known haunted houses. We enjoyed the haunted tour so much that our next vacation, the one we had this last spring, was for Salem, Massachusetts. We really didn't know what we were doing but I spent a lot of time mapping our trip on a road atlas and where and when we would stop for food and lodging along the way. This was a very long road trip for us, living in the Midwest as we do. And we found out it was Very Long. We spent our first night in a bed and breakfast in Lancaster County Pennsylvania. At the Blue Rock Bed and Breakfast in Lancaster County, Millersville PA. I don't mind advertising for them since it was a wonderful stay and the proprietors are very kind and good people. You will certainly get a very good and delicious breakfast in the morning and it was very clean and tidy. Next trip I would like to stay longer in that area. I'm fascinated by the Amish, and it is actually in my own heritage on my father's mother's side. We have some great recipes from my Amish relations like made-from-scratch egg noodles cooked in a chicken broth made in a pressure cooker. Now I'm hungry for my Grandma's chicken noodles!

The next night should be in Salem. Who knew the traffic outside of Boston would be so horrific! This was our first experience in New England and our first experience with this kind of traffic. So it took us two hours to travel less than five miles. The language coming out of my husband's mouth actually matched my own. Thank goodness for older children, two of whom are adults now. Because nothing could have stopped us from our angry expletives!

The Salem Inn was actually very nice, though not a true Bed & Breakfast. The breakfast was continental. But it was truly a "haunted Inn". I will share one story: on our first night, my husband was awakened by the sound of me rummaging through the drawers of the wardrobe in our room in the middle of the night and was becoming quite annoyed with me. Until he realized I was sleeping right next to him! He even heard the jingling of the metal hanging drawer knobs and footsteps pacing around the bedroom. Before that time, we did not realize we were staying in a Haunted Inn. The next day my son Douglas and youngest daughter Sarah and I happened to see a stack of journals in the fireplace lounge on the first floor and started to read some of the stories listed in there. There were several years of haunted experiences written inside those journals. This ended any chance of my youngest daughter to get a night's rest in that Inn. She craves the stories and is very interested in hearing them, but gets extremely frightened afterwards! She is a living contradiction in that respect. I consider myself very perceptive but I didn't experience any hauntings during our stay. Oh well.

We had a great time during our vacation and we went away thinking that the New England states are a very beautiful part of our country. But at the time, we were so sick of driving here and there; we became very crabby at each other. We even got tired of lobster after we went to the Lobster Shack in Salem and my older daughter Pam had a whole lobster. Before this event, we had only experienced lobster tails. She didn't realize until it was on her plate that the beady little eyes would still be on it and she didn't know how to crack it and where to start to eat it. It was the first time she had her fill of lobster.

The Plymouth Rock was a disappointment. I don't know why we all think it should resemble a noble, giant stone but it is actually very small and housed in a pavilion where people can no longer break off pieces of it. Apparently it started off bigger but I say, if it was impressive at one time, a lot of rock must have been chopped off! My Dad and I have picked off bigger rocks than that one when clearing our fields for planting!

Funny thing about husbands though, or maybe just mine. We had four licensed drivers in our vehicle, and one with a drivers permit. My husband would not relinquish the wheel. He complained loudly about how tired he was and how sore he was from driving. But he would not let me drive—our kids never volunteered—but I did quite often. But he wouldn't pull over or switch with me. It's all for the best, really. My husband needs to be in control, he's a terrible side-seat driver. If I drive, I usually tell him to close his eyes and take a nap because he drives me crazy! In my defense, I kept the Road Atlas and was the Navigator. When looking on side-streets for addresses like the local Wal-Mart in Salem for sundries and snacks or for the location of our Inns that we stayed at, thank goodness for my cell phone. Again, I'm a total fan of my IPhone. I've only had one for less than two years but I will never have another brand of cell phone, I love it so much!

So we decided, as a family, that if we ever decide to go to Salem or even to Maine, which we didn't get further than Kittery because of being tired of driving, we would fly. A twelve day trip and most of it was on the road. Our butts will thank us for paying airfare next time.

Enough about vacations, we do other things fun as a family like going to the Zoo or the Amusement Park (similar to Six Flags) or to the Science Museum or just on picnics to major parks or landmarks. The best times we have are when we are together, the five of us, no matter the age of the children. We laugh so hard we cry and we go away with new memories that warm us when we think of our love for each other and our precious time we spend together.

We went to the St. Croix River for a picnic in May this year. I packed a picnic lunch of everyone's favorite things: Southern fried Chicken strips, crab salad, fresh cut fruit, and homemade giant cookies. It was our first time at the river and after we ate, we walked down the steps and paths to the riverside and found some caves and abandoned bonfire pits. The cave was scary, with graffiti painted on the walls and old clothing scattered around the ground. My husband yelled at us that homeless people could be in there or drug addicts or maybe some satanic cult. We rushed out of there. But it was worth a laugh afterwards. And it was an inexpensive way to spend a day with the family.

With five of us we have our roles to play: Doug, my oldest, is the clown. He tries to keep everyone laughing with his sarcastic remarks while people watching (actually he is a very sensitive and polite individual) and making jokes, even about his family members. He can do perfect imitations of everybody! He is the life of the party and is very much needed on most outings to make it fun. Pamela is always the center of the show—she wore a dress everyday of our trip to Salem and if she wasn't wearing one, she was buying one. She is very aware of her looks and very aware of the looks she gets from others, though she tries hard to not flaunt herself, she is very pretty after all. Sarah, my youngest, constantly tries to make her brother laugh—he is her hero and she adores him—or she is trying to avoid her older sister because they mainly get on each other's nerves. Sad because I know they love each other very much. Hopefully they will grow out of this one day. I am the peacekeeper and the one trying to make everything fun. Also making sure everyone eats at regular intervals, this is very important! My husband is the old curmudgeon. I believe he does his best to try to make our children think he's incredibly old fashioned and out of the loop.

As our children grow older into adulthood and have their own lives and friends to spend time with, we must expect to spend less and less time together as a family. I look forward to having grandchildren some day and for my children to create their own family memories of vacations and trips to the zoo and picnics. But I'm in no hurry to marry them off yet. I will let them take their own time and cherish all our memories we can still create with just the five of us.

Chapter Ten

Funny thing about our jobs . . .

My husband and I started out our married lives together with the same job—we were both newly commissioned officers in the United States Army Reserve. We were also college students having yet to complete our degrees. My husband had a part time job in a jewelry store downtown where he was the engraver. But his degree was in Law Enforcement and we both knew that his goal was to be a police officer. Because we were planning a family, neither of us were inclined to be active Army officers, knowing that it would involve a lot of moving and coordinating since we were informed that being a married couple, we may have to be on separate Army posts. We certainly did not look forward to that and decided that the local State Army National Guard was a great place to fulfill our obligations to the US Government.

We work well together. We are very competitive. Our scores are always very close in a class room environment. Even when playing sports, like racquetball which we both love. Keeping score always led to fights so we got smart and decided to play by all the rules of the game but we would not keep score. We always had some kind of idea of who was winning since we would either have the serve or not depending on who scored the last hit. But we enjoyed it and it was still great exercise. Our awesome competitiveness would always stop passersby who would gather by the Plexiglas and watch us for a while. We were pretty proud of that. Of course, that was a few years ago and Ken's knees are too bad to play and we've both gained some weight. Not so awesome anymore. But we still have our memories.

So my husband became a cop in a major metropolitan city. I don't know what he'll do when he decides to retire. He's never really been a civilian. He went from active military to college where he met me and was in ROTC, then immediately into the National Guard after being commissioned as a 2nd

Lieutenant and then became a cop. Therefore now, he has little tolerance for what he calls "stupid people".

Stupid people can be anyone. All of our children grew up hearing their father say the phrase "I hate people . . ." I would tell him to shush up. He says he means it. What he means is that he has little tolerance for criminals—that is to say people who break the law, selfishness, ungratefulness, laziness, rudeness, foolishness, a lot of 'nesses. In fact, anything that makes us human and gives us those many faults that we all have. Some have more faults than others. He is a man of little tolerance, period. Really, he is a very good cop. He sees things as black or white. No gray areas. This was his training and he lives by this. He is not a different person, on or off the job. But he does allow me to be the confrontational one when he's off-duty. Unless he is very angry or upset, he will allow me to be the one to handle annoying phone calls or solicitors or leave a restaurant without ordering food because of poor service. That is until the last couple years. He has become more vocal off the job now and actually I'm very glad. I don't think it's always healthy to repress anger. It's not great for your blood pressure or your heart.

He has several stories he tells me about his day as a cop. Each day there is always a funny, strange, sad or just plain weird story about the strange things people do or say. Or even what people may name their children.

For a time my husband worked a part-time job, off-duty, for the Detox Center.

A nurse who worked there at one time worked for the County Medical Center in the maternity ward. This is not a cop story, more a nurse story, I suppose. One mother had twin boys and had no names picked out for them. So she decided to name them after her favorite food, which was Jell-O. So she named one Lemonjello (le-mahn-je-loh) and the other Orangejello (o-rahn-je-loh). Another lady believed that the hospital had already named her baby for her so this little girl's name is now Female (fe-mah-lee), since this was the name on the bassinet. Really . . . people. Actually, if you pronounce these names right, they sound kind of cool. I don't understand. My baby's names were picked out long before they were born.

My husband has some sad stories that he has to live with that also goes with the job. In his first few years as a rookie cop, an eight year old boy was walking along the railings of a bridge and fell off onto the railroad tracks below where a train immediately took both his legs off. My husband was the first to respond and he was mentally affected by this for a long time. He seriously thought about another career for a while. He has had several other sad experiences but even 20 years after this incident occurred, he still remembers this child. He has had several calls on "baby not breathing". These are also difficult for him. The other calls for a death, whether it's the elderly or drug over-doses or gun-shot victims are easier for him to deal with, though still sad. He is trained to deal with all of these but the children hurt him the most, as I would believe they would with most adults. But there are several stories with good endings too where he has resuscitated people not breathing and saved them from fires.

My husband has received several awards and accolades for his job performance, I am quite proud of him. But he refuses to climb any higher in his position. He doesn't want to be a sergeant or anything else but a street cop. He wants to remain hands-on, answering calls, helping people, and stopping wrong-doing first hand. He doesn't want a desk job. He scoffs at young people who train with him that tell him that they just want to sit at a desk and research crime. He believes that cops should all start out on the street and learn true human behavior in their daily lives, what the average Joe is capable of doing daily and to also help the people who need help.

When my husband worked a lot of third shifts ("dog watch",) he had a black binder. The binder was full of pictures of known prostitutes in the city. It was a very thick and full binder. Do not think prostitutes look like Julia Roberts in "Pretty Woman". They are all on meth or crack cocaine or some kind of drugs and look scabby and sad and very pathetic. None are attractive. So my husband had a black book full of women's pictures, so what? He also says things like "tonight, we're picking up prostitutes". These are the things you hear when you are the wife of a cop, I guess.

The worst days are always the holidays. Sad, but true, that the cops receive the most calls for Domestic Disturbance during Thanksgiving and Christmas. Families just can't get along when they are together under one roof. Fights always break out. How sad to have an annual event where the tradition is to call 911 each year. They should just set a place at the table for the cops at these homes and invite them immediately. That's just a joke, who would want that invitation? But it's sad when the children grow up in these families to expect that it is normal to have family fights break out. Do they grow up and do the same, a second generation of 911 Holiday callers? Well, why not? There are second and third generation drug abuser and alcoholics, second and third generation welfare families, as well as the second or third generation cop families, military families, farmers, etc.

My husband has arrested hundreds of people. It's frustrating for him that he re-arrested most of these people—recidivism is very high. He has also saved many people, whether they deserve saving or not, that is not for him to determine. Just a couple weeks ago he resuscitated a drug over-dose victim and saved his life. He also saved a naked, drunk man from a burning house. Did I say his job was fun? I don't think so.

My job has many similarities to my husband's job. He is a cop. I am a retail manager. Does anyone see the similarities? Only another retailer would know immediately what I'm referring to. There are domestic disturbances in the store, transients on the curb at the front doors, guns and knives (yes, really), drug users and drunks, and I'm not just talking about the customers, this applies to the employees as well! The difference is that I can't just haul them off to jail like my husband can when provoked or attacked. I just have to smile and say "Have a great day, come again soon!" And with the employees, there is a long process of "reasonable suspicion" and investigations. I wonder what ever happened to pride in your job. I think we're back to that second and third generation thing again. My parents taught me to take pride in my job and do it the best I know how. My mother always said, "Remember, your name is on your work. Make it the best and be proud of it always". My two children in the work force have that good work ethic. They don't miss work unless absolutely necessary, they do the best they can and achieve good evaluations and raises for their job performance. Actually, I think they're more scared of facing me than their manager if they do poorly. Mom always finds out.

But I believe the families with poor work ethic, the ones where the employee is always blaming someone else for their problems and poor job performance, the ones always absent, the ones who continuously harass co-workers and offend customers may have learned this from home. I am always a firm believer in good parenting, even if you are a new parent and don't really know what you're doing. Tough love is hard, you can't just let your children have whatever they want, waiting on them hand and foot; they don't learn and they need some discipline. Actually, I've found out through working in the public school system as a pera-professional, and in day-cares, that children love a routine and having structure is actually a comfort to them. Of course, I'm just throwing in my opinion again.

The guns and knives are true as well. Well, of course in retail you are going to have your thieves. I remember a day when we had a worker who was elderly, 82 years old in fact, and all he did was check receipts. He asked a young man as he was leaving the store for a receipt of a portable DVD player. The man said "here's my receipt" and pulled out a gun from his waist band and pointed it in the old man's face. Did he think the old man would physically take him down? What a little coward! All he had to do was run out the door; the old man couldn't chase him anyway. And I'm sure the coward thought that he pulled a good one on us because he got away with theft. Against an 82 year old frail man, now there's a real man. I detest thieves.

So every day I deal with customer problems and employee problems for 13 to 15 hours. Then I go home and deal with my teenager's problems and my adult children's problems. Then I listen to my husband's day because he has the need to vent and I'm always concerned and want to hear about his life away from me. And I also vent to him and he gets very frustrated with my day as well.

When I had the need for help, more help than just venting could do, I started going to the casino. I've written more about this in another chapter about mental therapy, but it is very true. Several housewives and mothers have hobbies, things that can take up their time and are fun to do. I love to read a good mystery, but I read too fast and then have no more books to read. I'm also very picky about the books I read. I hate a fiction book written in the first person (this book is in the first person!). I like to read books where you can get into the mind of all the characters, not just the hero or heroine's. Some are in the first person of several characters and this confuses me, who's telling the story now? Anyway, books are only good for reading before bed, on nights or days when I can't sleep. I crochet doilies, I crochet afghans, I paint, I bake, and I am trying to teach myself how to play the piano and guitar. And yet none of these things help me when my brain is going to explode from frustration and I need to escape! Hence, the casino was invented. I just need to watch my spending. It's very easy to lose track of time and money . . .

So my husband and I vent to each other about our day—thank goodness cell phones and text messaging was invented! I remember when, early in our marriage, my husband carried around a pager. If there was an emergency, I could page him and he would find the nearest phone and call me. I tried not to bother him too much, respecting the importance of his job and not wanting to get him in trouble. But now that there's texting (and the wonderful creation of an IPhone—I love my IPhone!!!), we can text each other about all our frustrations and little things that happen here and there. It's also a great way for us to keep in touch with our children. How handy is this Information and Technology Age that we are living in? I can't measure it but it is very handy in a busy world. But sometimes I know we would all just love to get away from it and hide from this busy world. Hiding is also so much harder to do today . . .

My husband both loves and hates his job. He gets very tired of the silly and stupid things people do but he still takes great pride in doing his job and he is very professional. Maybe some days he's not as courteous as others but we all really need to think about a cop's day. If we, the average citizen, get pulled over for a traffic violation, we need to realize that the officer may have just come from a burglary, a death, a fire, or anything. But he must still do his job and if he sees a violation, a law or rule or ordinance being violated, he must still stop the violator. So stop asking the cop "Don't you have any real criminals to chase?" because you're upset that you were caught. The idiots that use that phrase are always in the wrong, a hundred percent of the time.

If you drive 2 miles above the speed limit, you are still speeding. The cop can still give you a ticket. My husband has a rule. If you get a ticket, you get

No lecture. If you get a lecture, you get No ticket. He doesn't usually subject a violator to both, believing it is cruel and unusual punishment. But he still gets called an "asshole" most of the time. Or, in the case of women (and some men), they do a lot of crying. In fact, they cry more with the lecture than when getting the ticket. Who can guess? My husband gets so amazed that when he tries to be nice, most seem to get more upset. He just shakes his head at the world. No wonder he has such an opinion of people. He really would be happy living away from people on the top of a mountain in a shack. Except he needs a metropolitan area within 30 minutes if he requires a purchase of something. He is really very hard to please.

The divorce rate of police officers is very high, though according to fairly recent studies, not as high as actually perceived. *In the September 19th, 2010 issue of the Washington Post, an article by Ellen McCarthy entitled "Study breaks down divorce rates by Occupation"; she states that from the 2000 US Census, 16.35% of Americans who previously had been married listed they were now divorced or separated. She also states "Only 14.5% of Law Enforcement who had been married said the same. . . . varied widely across the profession: Just 12.5% of detectives were divorced, but 25.5% of fish and game wardens had broken up with a spouse." She continues with "Highest divorce rates were dancers and choreographers with divorce rates of 43.1%". The lowest rates were engineers, optometrists (4%), clergy (5.6%), and podiatrists (6.8%). She continues to say, later in the article, that this is not a complete picture. The study does not take into account that during the time between the Census reports, a person may be divorced and remarried. They would not have been counted in that group.

What I'm seeing in the difference between these divorce rates is the level of stress in the work place.

In another study I found in * "The Police Chief Magazine" volume LXXVI, no.1, January 2009, written by Gary Westphal, Chief of Police (retired) Mesquite, TX, and Linda Openshaw, Associate Professor of Social Work, Texas A&M University—Commerce; "According to the United States Department of Health and Human Services, National Center for Health Statistics, in 2005, marriages occurred at a rate 7.5% per 1000 people, while divorces occurred at a rate of 3.6% per 1000 people. In this article, they state that "past studies indicated that Law Enforcement Officers have one of the highest divorce rates when compared with other groups." Stress of the job was stated as a huge factor.

One more study I observed was one called * "Divorce Rates for Law Enforcement personnel: Another Myth bites the Dust" by Shawn P. McCoy and Michael G. Aamodt, Radford University from October 2008. I noticed their findings compared to the first article I mentioned from the Washington Post, using the 2000 US Census as their reference and that dancers and choreographers were again the highest among divorce rates. Well duh, think about their profession. Lots of hands on, don't you think? Lots of touching and intimacy, I can really see that there would be a lot of temptation in their work and there could definitely be a lot of fidelity issues.

So why do we have the perception that divorce rates among Law Enforcement officials are so high?

When searching the internet for related articles about law enforcement and divorce rates, one thing is common, and one header is prevalent. They repeatedly say: "Police and mental health; the Effects of stress on Police Officers; Is there a high suicide rate among Police Officers . . ."

I can only know that personally, within the metropolitan police force that my husband is a part of, the divorce rate is high. I also know that the remarriage rate is high as well. My husband has had several partners over his 23 years of being a cop for this particular city. I hope I'm quoting correctly that he has had eight different partners and I only know of one other that has been in the same marriage for almost as many years as my husband and I have been together.

I went into this marriage already knowing that my husband was going to be a cop, though he wasn't one yet. I knew he would have stressful days. I promised myself that I would always listen and be concerned for his safety—both mental and physical. I'm not perfect. My husband also knew he was going to have these days as well and has used me as a sounding board. He has been good about venting to me and he knows I am always on his side. Well, except those times he said "I hate people . . ." in front of the kids and I told him to "shush". Now he has several ways he can vent to me—in person, talking on the cell phone, or by texting on the cell phone. And he does. It still amazes me about the things people say and do in the world. Human nature, who can understand it?

*Articles and quotes taken from:

1. "Study breaks down Divorce rates by Occupation." The Washington Post, September 19, 2010 by Ellen McCarthy, Washington Post staff writer.
2. "Law Enforcement Healthy Marriage and Family Project." The Police Chief Magazine, vol LXXVI, no.1, January 2009 by Gary Westphal, Chief of Police (retired) Mesquite Texas and Linda Openshaw, Associate Professor of Social Work, Texas A&M University—Commerce.
3. "Divorce Rates for Law Enforcement personnel: Another Myth bites the dust." Study by Shawn P. McCoy and Michael G. Aamodt, Radford University, October 2008.

Chapter Eleven

Respecting Each Other . . .
Listening to Each Other

This chapter could also go along with the chapter about 51:49 ratio because both are talking about respect. But there's more to respect than just giving more or giving in.

When my husband and I were best friends, before we ever started dating each other, or even thinking about dating each other, we respected each other. We worked together, we studied together, we trained together side by side and we learned to have a great trust and camaraderie of each other. This has continued to this day, though it has changed several times throughout the years, as things do when people live and grow together.

I respect my husband's job and how well he does it and how seriously he takes his job. He respects my job and how much I've learned about the retail industry and the strides I've made to have the achievements and the position I've earned, even though it was a trade that I was never interested in as a youth.

The toughest part about respecting each other throughout our marriage is when raising our children and respecting what we have said to them at the time, whether we agree with each other or not.

Every parent has gone through the routine of the child going from one parent to another when trying to get the answer they want. If Mom says "no", go to Dad. Or worse yet, if Mom says "no", tell her Dad already said "yes". Or vice-versa. The trick is to be smarter than the child. Communicate enough with your spouse so that you are always on the same page. Or at the very least, communicate with Dad to verify the "yes" answer. Hey, I can override Dad if I have good reason to back it up. My husband will agree with me—most of the time he just says "Oh, I didn't know that . . ." I think that's a typical

Dad answer anyway. They just want to be left alone, just let him watch TV or read his book/newspaper, or play his computer game. I must only remember to not start a fight about it, like "you should have known", or "you should have asked me first", or the best one "why the @#$^&* did you tell her yes?!?!" Sometimes I am very unreasonable and my husband is thinking, again, "Sometimes marriage really sucks!" He would be right.

I don't know if this is true of all families, but I've noticed that some children feel more comfortable with one parent versus the other. In most families, it's usually the mom that the children will go to first. Mom usually has more patience, mom will usually say "yes" first, mom understands, and mom has more compassion. Not this mom. This mom is still learning patience; it's a toss-up between Dad and Mom about the rest.

But I do realize that our children will usually come to me first for two reasons. One is that Dad would rather they just ask me since I am usually more informed about school stuff and their personal stuff; he just lets me be that person. Let's just say that anyway. It's true that I've been involved in their school activities and volunteered for school events and chaperoning field trips. The girls would rather talk to me than their father about hormonal things (actually they don't like to talk to me about much of that either, unless they're sick) or just girl things. My son has only recently learned to communicate with his father now that he is an adult. Through most of my son's childhood, he and his father just clashed. His father never understood his son's likes and dislikes having been very different himself as a child. So my son just shared more with me. So the second reason is that they are just more comfortable coming to me. They've also learned over the years that Dad has them figured out and will just say "ask your Mom" which drives me CRAZY! My husband knows that he won't make a mistake with an answer I won't be happy with and it also lets him off the hook. Wives, husbands learn this from us, so beware! If you argue about a "yes" or "no" answer with your husband due to a question from your children stop yourself and let your husband decide. Then maybe you won't get the "just ask your mother" answer. And maybe not. Who can understand men?

When it comes to respecting each other, it is even more important with regards to how we treat each other in front of the in-laws. They watch you very closely. The good ones want you to always show care and concern for each other and worry when things don't look good. The bad ones revel in your open fighting and love the discontent. I've found that unhappy people want all people to be unhappy. It makes them crazy when they see happiness. Why should they be happy when I'm not? Why should she have what I don't? I want to have what everyone else has and not have to work for it. Better watch out, I'm going down a different political path now and must stop. Time for a new paragraph . . .

My husband has always acted differently when around his family. He acts different, he talks different. Maybe it's because he was always the baby, the youngest brother, I don't know. I suppose they treated him differently as well. I don't know that he realizes that he behaves differently but I didn't at first. All I knew as a young bride was that my new husband had a difficult time expressing himself to his family, a difficult time standing up to his family. He still does. He cannot speak reasonably or logically with them. He skips a step, he is quiet and then when he has had enough of their pettiness or their accusations, he explodes. He becomes almost irrational. I realize now that it comes from many, many years of holding his feelings inside and not expressing any of them. Too many years of anger building up that he cannot speak to them with reason. Admittedly, they are difficult people to reason with. I can proudly say that he does not have a problem bottling up his feelings with me. I've chipped away at him through persistent nagging for 26 years that now he talks just to shut me up. I'm not a fool; I know how my husband thinks. True, we're still working on this one.

No matter what my husband's behavior may be or what he may or may not say to them, I will quietly support him. The key word is "quietly". They are still his family and no matter how I may feel about what's going on at the time, I must remember to not say too many negative things. It is one thing for a person to feel anger at their own family and speak out because of it but it's another thing for an outsider to do the same. Even though I know I'm his wife, even 26 years later I am very careful how I phrase things in regards to my in-laws. We cannot forget that our children are part of both families and they should not always hear only the negative. When I reminisce about the grandparents to my children, I try very hard to remember the good things and talk about them. They hear enough and remember enough about the negative without me adding more to it.

My husband does the same with me and my family—to a certain extent. He still may say too much of his opinion of someone or possibly their actions and I may resent his remarks and yell at him to stop it. And he will. But then his anger is against me, not my family, since I yelled at him. Oh well. There aren't too many situations where my husband has negative comments to say about my immediate family. He cares deeply about my three sisters and their spouses and their children. He loves my parents like his own and my Grandmother is very dear to him. So for the most part we speak about them with love and concern. There are some instances, however, that require some long debates afterwards and since I love my family too much, I will not go into them.

But I can mention quickly that my husband loves to go deer hunting and has not done so for the last 15 years at least. It is because he does not get along with my Uncle and it is a very distinct personality clash. My husband is not a tolerant man (I've stated this before, haven't I?) and so would rather miss the hunting than to be around my Uncle. My Uncle knows this so I can write about it and not feel that I am giving anything away by it. This is an argument that my husband and I have had for more than the last 23 years since they first began hunting together. "They" are my father, uncle, husband, and various other hunters in their party mainly consisting of other city cops, county deputies and jailors that my father worked with, my Uncle's best friend, and for a few years my husband's oldest brother.

Our continuous argument over deer hunting season is that my husband keeps saying how much he misses it and I keep telling him it's his own fault. He is welcome to hunt with my father every year, my Uncle has no personal problem with my husband—he treats all people the way he treats my husband. It's my husband's own choice that he misses out. But neither do I want my very sensitive husband to be miserable and unhappy during his vacation time. He is what he is and I cannot change him so I only argue with him out of principle now. And anyway, I don't do it in front of my parents. The sad part is that my husband misses seeing my Aunt Setsuko, who is my mother's only sister, who he likes very much because of course she cooks for him! My mother and her sister are both wonderful cooks, especially of Japanese food, which my husband is very fond of. I missed her too so now I just go to my parent's house without him—even though it is a 6 ½ hour drive one way. And I have learned to care about my Uncle which was not easy for me when I was a young girl. His personality can be very difficult and it took many years for me to understand him but now I know it's only because he's from Texas. Just kidding Uncle Aub!

My husband and I have a system that we've learned over the years. If there's something or someone that bothers us or we don't like them, we simply avoid them. That's all. For the most part, we really keep to ourselves. It's been several years since I've had good friends or neighbors come to our house for dinner or a cookout. That's largely because of my horrible work schedule and also my husband's long work days and changing work rotations. So I guess we've become more like hermits than ever before. We certainly enjoy our Super Bowl Party that we still have every year in February with the same group of friends that we've had for the last 15 years, ever since we got our first big screen TV. It's become an annual event. I love to entertain but I know my husband would rather have a quiet evening to relax so we don't entertain too often. In fact, you could probably count on one hand how many times we entertain in our home per year. So I respect my husband's need for privacy and he respects my need to entertain the few times that I ask him.

My husband also allows me to go out for dinners or drinks (or both) with my girl-friends as well. He only requires that I let him know what hours I'm keeping and I tell him where we're going, if I know. At one time he used to stay up for me. He doesn't anymore. In fact, he goes to bed earlier and earlier each night, it seems. Sometimes as early as 6:30pm! I told him that I know we're getting older but we're not that old yet! He says he's going to read for a while but I know that I'll find him, 5 or 10 minutes later, with his glasses still on snoring loudly. I'll take his glasses off and he may or may not wake up. It's true that when he works he gets up at 4:00am and even on his days off he sometimes can't sleep much later than that. So I suppose by 6:30pm he may be very tired. He just tells me he's getting old. He has been saying that to me since the year we got married. He was 26 and I had just turned 22. He is almost exactly 4 ½ years older than me so he feels old and always says he's old. I ask him now if he thinks 26 years is old. He says no, why should he think 26 is old? Because you said you were old when you were 26! He says that he *was* old when he was 26. Whatever! It's true, he really knows how to get me going, another point of contention that we've had for just as long.

This chapter is called Respecting each other, Listening to each other. The last part is the most difficult. I can truthfully say that I hear every word my husband says when we are fighting or arguing. But do I really listen to him? Sometimes I know I don't. It depends on my mood at the time. It also depends on if I feel he is listening to me or not.

I really hate when I tell my husband about an event or an anniversary or birthday and he says he never knew about it. I only reminded him several times for several days or even weeks before hand. He does not listen sometimes when I'm just talking about normal, everyday things. My daughter's Choir Concerts are now reserved seating tickets to pre-purchase and I've been telling him this was going to happen since last spring. He had a fit and was upset about why we had to pay for seats for a Choir Concert when we never had to pay for the older children's concerts. I had already explained to him about the parent's thinking it was a good idea, it is only a minor cost of $2 per seat, and it would also ensure that you would have a seat instead of standing in long lines. If my husband had listened when I warned him for months ahead of time that this was a good thing and was going to happen in the fall, we would not have had the drama afterwards.

It is not easy to teach ourselves how to listen. It was hard enough for me to teach my husband how to talk to me. How do I teach him how to listen? But it begins with wanting to listen. So it doesn't pay to talk to each other if both parties are not willing to listen. When I think my husband is ready to listen, then I will talk to him. I have always told my children, when they have to ask Dad something difficult, to wait until he is home from work, supper is done, and he is in comfy mode on the couch in front of the TV. Then, when he is relaxed and happy, drop the bombshell on him. He may or may not overreact. It's really a 50/50 chance, depending on the situation or the question asked.

It's the same with having serious talks and discussions concerning our relationship with each other. I can wait, sometimes, for a good time to talk to my husband about something concerning our relationship, or my job, or our children when I think he is ready to listen. But it's harder for me to know when I'm also ready to listen to his response. It's pretty selfish of me to just think he's the only one that needs to listen. If I'm not ready to listen to whatever his initial response may be, then one of two things may happen. I will either end the conversation with "you never listen to what I'm really trying to say!" and not giving him a chance to explain himself, or he will end the conversation with the same phrase. Then it's a lose/lose situation. No one is the winner of those conversations.

I've said this before and I'll say it again, I am not a patient person. I am only recently attempting to master the "wait for my husband to be ready to talk" trick in our marriage. Being prepared to listen is my next hurdle. I've only scratched the surface on that concept. But I'm willing to concede that it is an important aspect of a good and/or difficult conversation.

You see, it's an easy thing to sit and say what the right thing to do in a relationship is. It's another thing to put it into practice. My husband and my relationship together has never been stagnant. You could compare us to a pool of water. The pool runs deep. But there are lots of ripples that can disturb the water. The ripples are okay, little things that we work out each day. We must be careful that the ripples do not turn into waves, so we must keep control of hurt feelings by talking and smoothing out the ripples before they become waves. To be aware of this is a constant challenge in our marriage. It's all about thinking about the feelings and respecting the feelings and having consideration of the feelings—of your partner. Then you must be willing to Listen to their feelings. Listening to their feelings without talking about your own at the same time is very difficult. If my husband is talking about how he feels about something and I respond with how I feel about it, we get nowhere. Then we are both talking and no one is listening. I've found out that at these times it's best to just stop talking and walk away, to continue the discussion later when we've both thought about things for a while. Being careful about how I walk away is important too. It's best to just say "let's talk more later . . ." as I walk away.

My husband and I have made a lot of mistakes in our marriage, mistakes where we've disrespected each other, hurt each other with spiteful words, thrown things at each other (actually only me throwing things at him), and given each other the silent treatment. We've always made up because we love each other deeply, it's what always brings us back together, and it's what makes us want to stay together. We meant it when we said forever. I recommend that before anyone marries, think about forever. Forever is a serious thing and a great commitment. But it's the most wonderful thing in the world when it's meant for two people. I wish you all to find your forever someone, or work with your current someone on your forever, together.

In Conclusion . . .

I don't really have a conclusion, we're still living the dream, daily. We continue to fight with each other and learn from each other. But everything that happens here, in my household, happens out of love. This has passed to our children, who carry on our tradition of care and respect, hard work and love for each other.

There's no conclusion. Only continuing to work on forever, in this world and the next.

www.ingramcontent.com/pod-product-compliance
Lightning Source LLC
Chambersburg PA
CBHW020337290526
45785CB00005B/2062